# THE
# LIVES
## OF
# NINE
# CATS

# THE
# LIVES
## OF
# NINE
# CATS

William O. Foss

Illustrations by Julie Neher

**HAMPTON ROADS**
PUBLISHING COMPANY, INC.

Hampton Roads Publishing Company, Inc.
891 Norfolk Square
Norfolk, VA 23502
Or call: (804)459-2453
    FAX: (804)455-8907

If you are unable to order this book from your local bookseller, you may order directly from the publisher. Call 1-800-766-8009, toll-free.


Cover design by Patrick Smith

ISBN 1-878901-15-X

10 9 8 7 6 5 4 3 2 1

Printed in the United States of America

# Contents

To the memory of Dulcie

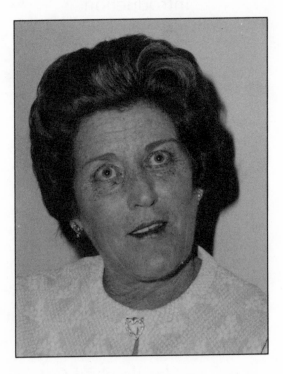

# Introduction

Authors write books for many different reasons. This book was written because my wife Dulcie asked me to write her a book about the cats that had given us so much pleasure over the years.

What could I write about cats that had not already been written? Cats are cats, and most cats do what other cats do. I was stymied.

Write about their personalities, said Dulcie.

Personalities?

She was right, of course. Just as each of us humans has our own personality, so do cats have their own personalities—behavioral characteristics, if you please.

Cats are remarkable creatures. They are self-reliant, independent, sensitive; and they are delightful, intriguing, lovable pets.

Although this book was meant to be *our book*, and not a bid for public favor, Dulcie left this world before it was finished.

Yet, gentle reader, please share it with us.

William O. Foss
October, 1992

# 1.
# MY FIRST CAT. . .
# AND GRANDFATHER'S CAT

Memories of my childhood days in Norway have dimmed over the years, yet there are certain events that are permanently etched in my mind, and among them are vivid recollections of my life with Sonja, my first cat.

Sonja, a black and white cat, and I were both brought up and loved by my paternal grandparents, Master Carpenter Otto Fosshaug and his wife Hilda, who lived in the town of Hyggen, nestled in the Hyggen Bay of the Drammensfjord.

My grandparents came by me upon the death of my mother Alma, who, like my father Hans, had immigrated from Norway to America. Being born in the Dorchester section of Boston, I was just a toddler when my mother passed away. My father, energetic and strong-minded, who had Americanized the family name to plain Foss, apparently felt that a little child would be a hinderance to him earning a living in the United States and decided that I would be better off being raised by his parents in Norway. I would not see my father again until I was fourteen.

Grandfather Fosshaug was a robust man with a head of short-clipped gray hair and a neatly trimmed moustache, who carried his body in a ramrod position like a soldier he had once been. A no-nonsense type of man, his booming voice would command the immediate attention of man or beast whenever he spoke. Yet for all the outward appearance of Viking fierceness, Otto Fosshaug was a gentle, caring man, respected by all with

*Grandfather Otto Fosshaug holds Veslepus (Little Puss) while my Norwegian family poses for an Easter photograph. The ladies are Aunt Torbjørg Eriksen (her husband Alf was the photographer) and Grandmother Hilda Fosshaug.*

whom he came in contact.

Grandmother Fosshaug, a quiet, kind lady, a bit on the chubby side, wore her beautiful gray hair in an upsweep, held neatly together on the top of her head in a bundle pierced with a comb. She seemed always to be wearing a long white apron that reached well below her knees. The apron was very useful. Taking hold of the lower edges of the apron, she would shape it into a basket in which she would carry kindling wood for the kitchen stove, apples and pears she picked in the fruit orchard, eggs she collected in the hen house, flowers she cut from her favorite garden, and a multitude of other things she felt could be properly toted in her favorite garment.

Grandmother usually didn't wear an apron when she visited neighbors, but one summer day she went off rather hurriedly still wearing the apron. When she returned from her visit she came to Grandfather's workshop, where she called for our immediate attention.

"I have something we need around here," she announced. It was obvious she was carrying something in her apron. Grandfather put away his plane, picked up a curled wood shaving and began chewing on it.

He often chewed on wood shavings or wood chips, especially when he was cogitating.

"What have you there?" he asked.

"A mouser!" Grandmother replied with a glee as she opened her apron, releasing a small black and white cat.

"Meow! Meow! Meow!" the cat cried as it jumped to the ground, circling three pairs of human legs in search of a safe place.

Grandfather grunted disapprovingly. It didn't look like a mouser to him. Besides, the mice around here were too quick for the cat and the rats would surely gnaw the cat's tail.

Grandmother disagreed with Grandfather's pessimistic assessment of the cat's mousing ability. It will grow into a good mouser, she asserted.

"Who is going to take care of the cat?" Grandfather asked.

"William!" proclaimed Grandmother.

"It's my cat?"

"Yes," said Grandmother. "Now you can have your own pet."

While I was exuberant and literally jumping for joy, I did have enough presence of mind to properly thank my grandparents for presenting me with this wonderful gift. "*Mange takk*—many thanks," I said, bowing my head and shaking their hands. Proper manners were to be practiced at all times, even among family members, according to the social standards of my grandparents. As I recall, good conduct and proper manners were a requirement of all Norwegians, children and grownups alike.

Looking back to those childhood days, I now believe that there was no disagreement between my grandparents about the need for a mouser. I am now sure that they had schemed to get me the cat. Good acting for a couple of amateurs.

"Here Kitty, Kitty!" I called as I got down on my knees to reach out for the scared animal. Boy, wasn't that the cutest little cat. "Don't be afraid, Kitty. Come here."

The cat had some qualms about being taken up by a child. It sidestepped me quickly when I tried to grab it. "Come here!" I demanded. The cat sought refuge under Grandmother's skirt and apron.

"Don't scare the poor thing," she admonished, and reached down and gently lifted the cat up to her bosom. She patted the cat and it seemed to calm down.

After cradling the cat like a little baby and talking sweetly to it, Grandmother handed the cat over to me. "Now, handle it gently and you two will get along fine." The cat cried several mournful meows as I held it tightly in my arms, but it calmed down after I stroked it gently and reassured it that everything was going to be all right. The cat seemed to understand what I said because it stopped wiggling and relaxed in my arms.

The cat would truly be my first pet. While I had two favorites among the denizens in my grandparents' hennery, you couldn't pet them, or talk to them, or love them like you could a cat. Until the cat arrived on the scene, I was taken by the antics of a brown-red-and-black-colored rooster named Finnbeck and a white hen named Fia. Finnbeck and Fia were the Norwegian names for the famed comic strip characters Jiggs and Maggie. Finnbeck properly carried out his role as a rooster of the flock should; Fia, whose slender body made her look like a beauty model when compared to her corpulent

*Barefooted, I pose with Sonja, my first cat, at the home of my grandparents in Hyggen, Norway.*

and unkempt sister hens, strutted around like a high society snob. She seemed always to be aloof around the other hens, even at feeding time. When the hens hurried to the feeder, Fia would bide her time, waiting for the person feeding them to place the food near her. Maybe Fia wasn't a snob; perhaps she was just spoiled.

The cat Grandmother had brought home to me was mostly black but with a pretty white face and black ears. The tail was all black, and there were white spots on the front paws and legs. The belly was somewhat white. It was a beautiful cat.

The cat had to be given a name, but first we had to determine its gender. Grandfather made an examination and established that it was a female cat.

A girl cat. So now I had to decide on a good Norwegian girl's name for my first pet. At first I thought I would name the cat after one of my girl classmates at school, but I wasn't particularly keen on girls; sports heroes and explorers like Roald Amundsen were my main interest at that time.

Aunt Torbjørg, who was visiting from Oslo, suggested that the cat be named Laila, after the heroine in a popular novel about a Lapp girl who lived with her reindeer-herding family in the harsh environment in Finnmark in northern Norway.

Laila sounded like a good name, but what about naming the cat after Sonja Henie, Norway's and perhaps the world's best-known female figure skater? The previous winter my uncle Henrik had taken me to Oslo to watch a speed skating championship at the Frogner Stadium. Sonja Henie, who had just won another world title, appeared and put on a dazzling exhibition of her figure skating prowess. Yes, Sonja would indeed be a fitting name for my cat, who was just as agile and athletic as Sonja the figure skater. So I made an important decision; my cat would be named Sonja.

Although Sonja was a free-roaming cat, she was provided with a special bedding, a cloth-covered wooden box, in Grandfather's storage shed where he kept a variety of items, including neatly stacked wood cut for use in the stoves. The shed was in the middle of a large outbuilding that housed Grandfather's workshop at one end and a neat and comfortable outdoor toilet on the opposite end. Sonja would never be lonesome for human companionship; there would always be some traffic in her area.

The storage shed was Sonja's bedroom, but during midsummer time, when the sun would remain in the sky for nearly all the twenty-four hours, it was difficult to get any Norwegians—grownups, children, or animals— to go to bed at a decent time. In the winter time, when cold weather and layer upon layer of snow would make it difficult for man and beast to get around, Sonja was reprieved from staying in the shed and spent most of the winter living in the house, near a warm stove.

Grandmother's intuition that my cat would be a good mouser was correct. Not only did Sonja catch her share of mice, but often she would lay her dead victims at the back door for special viewing. With her tail pointed upward, she strutted around the dead animal like a warrior cat proudly displaying her war trophy. We would, of course, compliment her on her great deed.

One nice spring day my grandparents entertained the district postmaster and his wife in the glass-enclosed sun room, which faced south and overlooked the Hyggen Bay. It was a rather warm day so the outside door leading to the sun room was left open.

Sonja, who had just captured a small field mouse, seeing the door open, offered to show her latest prey to the visitors and my grandparents. The poor mouse, stunned but still wiggling, got loose and scampered under the skirt of the postmaster's wife. The woman, apparently having great fear of rodents, let out an ear-piercing shriek, threw her hands wildly into the air, flew up from the table, and in the process knocked over Grandmother's cake dish. The mouse dashed out of the room with Sonja in hot pursuit.

Grandmother was thoroughly embarrassed by Sonja's antics and apologized profusely to the woman, who was almost overcome with apoplexy. Grandmother treated Sonja as a *persona non grata* for several weeks after that incident.

While Sonja had total mastery over the local mice, she was unable to cope with certain other members of the rodent family, namely squirrels. Whenever she spotted a squirrel on the ground, her ears would lie back in a menacing manner, her tail would swish from side to side, and, at what she thought was the proper moment, she would leap toward the squirrel. There was, of course, never a proper moment for Sonja to attack and catch a squirrel. The bushy-tailed squirrels were well aware of Sonja's presence, and, at the moment Sonja leaped, the squirrels, using their strong hind legs, scampered quickly up a tree, safely out of Sonja's reach. Sonja would cry out a couple of anguished meows to vent her frustration, while the teasing squirrel would chitter gleefully from the safety of a high tree limb.

Cats like milk and fish, and both of these commodities were part of the solid diet offered by Grandmother Fosshaug. Sonja seemed always to be on hand whenever I brought home a couple of pails of fresh milk from the neighboring farm. She would follow me into the kitchen, and Grandmother would dutifully fill her saucer with fresh milk. Sometimes one pail might bump against my leg, causing some milk to spill over the side. Whenever Sonja noticed the spilled milk, she would reach up and try to lick it off the side of the pail.

Fish was plentiful in the Drammensfjord, and I often contributed to the family dinner by catching a variety of fish with my simple fishing gear, a pole, hook, line and sinker. The hook was baited with the meatiest worms that I dug up in the chicken yard. Sonja never went fishing with me, but one day I saw her catch a good-sized trout. Honest!

There was a large brook running alongside Grandfather's property and spilling into the Hyggen Bay. The brook was important in our daily lives because it provided us with fresh water. We were blessed with electricity and telephone service (we had one of those crank-up telephones into which you conversed with the operator before contacting your party), but so-called city water service was not available in my youth.

One spring day I had made my way across the brook—jumping over and stepping on small and large and oddly shaped rocks—over to Captain Jensen's property. Jensen was a retired sea captain who had lost a leg when his sailing vessel, carrying a cargo of naphtha, blew up and sank at high sea. The peg-legged captain ran a small farm and was friendly with my grandfather.

He liked to tell sea stories and once gave me a sliver crown for helping him stack hay.

While exploring near the brook on Jensen's farm, I came upon a batch of wild strawberries. They were juicy and delicious. I wanted to pick some strawberries to take home to my grandparents, but I didn't have any container to carry them in. Then I spotted an area covered with tall, wiry grasses near the edge of the brook. I pulled some of these grasses and threaded them with strawberries, much like a jeweler threads pearls on a string. When I finished picking and threading strawberries I headed back toward the brook.

Grandfather had built a small shed near the brook, where Grandmother could store her washing equipment and soaps. Outside the shed hung a large black iron kettle in which she boiled the laundry. Locating the wash shed a short distance from the brook made it easier for Grandmother to haul water to the kettle.

When I approached the wash shed, I noticed Sonja sitting motionless near the edge of the brook, staring intently into the water. The brook was a little wider and deeper at that particular spot, and I could see speckled brook trout swimming in the clear, cool water. Sonja was fascinated with the fish swimming close to the edge of the brook. The trout seemed to be unaware of Sonja's presence, or else they were teasing her because they knew that cats didn't like water.

Then I noticed that Sonja's ears were laid back and her black tail was thumping, both signals that she was roused to displeasure or angry at the playful brook trout.

Suddenly, like a flash of lightning, her right paw struck the water, her sharp claws hooking a speckled trout that landed several feet in the grass behind her. The trout wiggled desperately, trying to escape Sonja's constant jabbing with her sharp claws.

"Hey! Sonja! You caught a fish!" I yelled. "Hurrah! Hurrah!"

Quickly I skipped over the rocks in the brook and joined Sonja in celebrating her prized fish catch. I moved it farther away from the edge of the brook so it wouldn't wiggle back into the water.

With Sonja trailing behind me, I carried her trout

*My Norwegian Sonja catches a brook trout.*

and my strawberries into Grandmother's kitchen, where we both triumphantly displayed the spoils of our adventures. Grandmother was particularly pleased with Sonja's catch.

"Now you see that Sonja is not only a good mouser, but also a good fisherman," she said. Then she rewarded Sonja with a savory fried trout, while my grandparents and I enjoyed a dish of cream and wild strawberries.

Ever since they were first domesticated by the ancient Egyptians, cats have been associated with mysticism and the supernatural. As a child I heard folk tales about cats being associated with witches. It was said that if you listened carefully when the witches rode the skies on their brooms to their annual meeting in the mountains, you could hear their cats meowing. Or was that the sounds of the wind? Sometimes witches would turn themselves into cats. If you saw a cat at night with shiny yellow eyes, you'd know right away that you had met up with a visiting witch.

Among my favorite readings in my childhood were Norwegian folk stories collected by Peter Christian Asbjørnsen and Jørgen E. Moe. Their collections included stories about kings, princesses and ordinary people, as well as trolls, bears, foxes, cows, goats, and, of course, cats. I remember a story about a gluttonous tabby that ate everything in sight and another story about an inebriated mouse that talked himself out of being caught and eaten by a cat.

Cats also played a part in Norse mythology—stories of the gods and goddesses honored by the Vikings. One of the Norsemen's goddesses, Freyja, who helped people in affairs of love, was said to travel in a chariot drawn by cats.

Then there was Nissen, the good-natured elf, a little old man wearing a gray suit and red cap, who was the Norwegian household spirit. Nissen, who usually lived in the barn—Grandfather's storage shed, in our case—was friendly with the family cat and preformed helpful services when the family was sleeping. Tradition had it that if you were good to Nissen he would reward you with good luck during the year. Since he lived with the household cat, it behooved you to also treat the cat kindly throughout the year. Like most Norwegian children, I was led to believe that the little elf Nissen was for real. My grandparents played their parts well in carrying out the old customs.

One custom was to share the Christmas cheer with all living things, including barnyard animals, birds and, of course, Nissen. The birds were treated with sheaves of oats, which were placed on poles, on window sills, and in trees. On Christmas Eve, a special family day in Norway, Sonja was given a saucer of cream, and Grandmother ladled out a dish of creamy rice porridge for Nissen. I dutifully placed the dish of porridge and a wooden spoon in the storage shed so Nissen could partake in the holiday celebrations, The next morning I would find the dish empty and wiped clean. Amazing!

As a free-roaming cat, Sonja had many suitors. Grandfather was not pleased when other felines would come upon the property, so he would immediately shoo them away. But as Nature would have it, Sonja became pregnant. Grandfather's vigilance had been for naught.

When it became time for Sonja to give birth, Grandmother had Grandfather build a special box for Sonja. The box, filled with layers of rags and warm clothing, was placed in the entryway to the kitchen. Grandmother wanted the cat to be comfortable when she gave birth.

I don't remember the number of kittens in Sonja's litter, but only one her offsprings was a black and white kitten. It was almost identical to Sonja—black ears, white face, black tail and white feet. There the resemblance ended—it was a male cat.

Since Grandmother served as postmistress of the town of Hyggen, she had let all interested parties know that Sonja had a litter of lovely kittens and that they would be given away when they were weaned from their mother. At the proper time, all but one, the black and white kitten, were sent out for adoption. Some of the kittens met their new owners when the owners came to the post office to pick up their mail.

Sonja's male offspring was different than the other kittens. Besides being smaller than the others, the little black and white male cat appeared to be a weak, sick animal, with constantly runny eyes. And its hind legs were abnormally long, like the rear legs of a hare or rabbit. Uncle Kåre, who lived nearby, joked that Sonja probably had mated with a rabbit. Grandmother scolded him for making such a cruel joke.

Grandfather showed immediate concern for the welfare of the little ailing kitten. He would lift it tenderly and gently cradle it in his arms so it could be comforted by the warmth of his body. He patted it and talked to it in a hushed voice like a mother talking fondly to her baby.

At first the kitten was nameless, but when Grandfather began calling it *Veslepus*—Little Puss—everyone agreed that that was a most appropriate name for the small, helpless animal.

Grandfather Fosshaug was a strong, determined man—some might have called him a stubborn man—who worked relentlessly to achieve the goals he set for himself. He now set himself the goal of nursing ailing Veslepus into a strong, healthy cat.

In the days of my youth there were no veterinarians or animal hospitals around to take care of ailing animals, but Grandfather applied the best homemade remedies to transform a sickly kitten into a sprightly and healthy cat. Using an antiseptic solution made from boric acid, Grandfather cleared up Veslepus' runny eyes, and the little cat gained strength by eating his mixture of cream and mashed meat.

Sonja also did her best to comfort her ailing offspring. As cats bathe themselves by licking their fur, Sonja seemed to make an extra effort to bathe Veslepus and let him cuddle and sleep curled up against her soft and warm belly. Long after Veslepus had passed the normal suckling stage for kittens and was eating food and drinking milk like a grown cat, Sonja would let him draw milk from her teats. But sometimes she would slap at him and chase him away, as if she was saying, "Enough! You're a big boy now."

Veslepus turned out to be a healthy animal, playful and lovable, and the elongated hind legs were not detrimental to his well-being; rather they enhanced his charm and enabled him to jump higher and run faster.

Grandfather doted over Veslepus, and the little cat reciprocated the affection by following Grandfather wherever he went, helping him in the workshop (i.e., playing with wood shavings), rubbing up against his legs, and purring loudly when Grandfather fondled him.

While Veslepus would explore the nooks and crannies of the Fosshaug property, he was never far away from the back door, the usual entrance to the home. Grandfather did not want Veslepus to roam the land, so he did his best to train the cat to stay close to home. He developed a special call—"Pssh! pssh! pssh! pssh!—a sort of loud wind-blown sound, which usually brought the cat running, meowing his acknowledgement, "I'm coming, I'm coming; here I am!" At night, Grandfather would make certain the little cat was placed safely in the storage shed, where he bedded down in a well-padded wooden box. In winter time, both cats would be sheltered in the warm family house.

When I left Norway in the early 1930s to be reunited with my father in the land of my birth, the strange and unknown United States of America, I was saddened to leave my grandparents. But I went away with the knowledge that I had been a most fortunate child to have been raised and loved by the two most wonderful and compassionate people in the world. I am sure that the first two cats in my life, Sonja and Veslepus, would agree.

# 2.
# The Ship's Cat

It was a cool, breezy fall day in 1937, and there I was, bewildered and humbled, just out of Navy boot camp, standing at attention in front of two weather-beaten, dungaree-clad chief petty officers, on the well deck of the *USS Jacob Jones*, a flush-deck, four-stack destroyer, tied up alongside a pier at the Naval Operating Base in Norfolk, Virginia.

The chiefs, one a chief boatswain's mate, the other a chief machinist's mate, were eyeing eight young, confused and uneasy sailors, who were about to be given their first assignments after reporting for duty aboard their first honest-to-goodness warship. The chiefs looked us over like farmers viewing cattle at a livestock auction, trying to pick the best of the herd.

Someone else was also looking us over.

A brown tabby.

The cat, sitting between the two chiefs, was eyeing the novice sailors with obvious curiosity. Its head moved from one sailor to another, then from the shiny black shoes to the blue flattop hats, as if it were giving the young men its own Navy personnel inspection.

The chief machinist's mate, a short stocky man, wiped his hands with an oily rag and barked, "Who wants to be a snipe?"

Three boys raised their hands.

"Step over here," he commanded. "I need one more."

Not knowing what a snipe was or did, I kept my mouth shut and hands down. ("Snipe" turned out to be Navy jargon for a member of the ship's engineering

14

department.)

"You!" the chief growled, fingering at one of the boot sailors, who dutifully placed himself alongside the other snipes. The chief then marched the sailors aft to acquaint them with the engine room and their new duties.

The chief bosun, a tall, broad-shouldered man, his hat slightly cocked, with hands stuck in the dungaree hip pockets, leaned forward and studied his frightened subjects. His square jaw protruded as he spoke his first words: "Welcome to the Jakie's deck force."

While we all remained silent, I was pleasantly surprised by the bosun's greeting. At boot camp we had been subjected to a constant barrage of morning and night drills, yelling and shouting, and demeaning insults by a grumpy chief, who was determined to break our backs before we could become sailors.

Then, in a booming voice, the chief bosun bellowed, "Do you know how to swim?" We all answered that we could. I was sure that he wasn't considering us for the ship's swimming team.

"Good. After you change into your dungarees, you're going over the side to paint the ship."

Then he picked up the cat and patted it, dismissed us, and turned us over to the care of a petty officer who would introduce us to our living quarters and explain the routine of life in our new home.

As the petty officer led us away, the chief, with the cat nestled in his arms, asked if we liked cats. We mumbled that we did.

"Good. This is Philbert, the ship's cat. He's our lucky charm. I don't want to see or hear of any of you mistreating him."

I was to learn that Philbert had VIP status second to none, except for the skipper. For example, Philbert could roam freely around the bridge (which was out of bounds for most sailors, except for assigned watchstanders), even to the point of taking a nap in the captain's chair while the old man was on the bridge.

As for sleeping, the cat could sleep anywhere he wanted and usually did. The chief bosun had made him a special hammock which was rigged behind one of the smoke stacks and above the warm engine room. Philbert would take (cat)naps in the hammock when the weather was pleasant, but he preferred doing his solid sleeping the crew quarters of the deck force. The cat usually bedded down on an empty bunk vacated by a watchstander or a sailor ashore on liberty. When the sailor returned to his bunk, he would, depending on his like or dislike for cats, throw the cat out of his bunk, gently move it onto another empty bunk, or (if he really liked felines) go to sleep cuddling the cat. Philbert never seemed to mind this extra attention.

As a VIP, Philbert had his "personal" toilets. The ship-fitter had made him two sheet metal litter boxes filled with sand. One box was located topside near his hammock, while the other was near the bottom of the ladder leading down to the forward crew's quarters. It was the duty of the captain of the head to keep the litter boxes clean and filled with fresh sand. (Landlubbers need to know that the "head" is Navy jargon for toilet or wash room, and that "captain of the head" is the individual selected to provide janitorial service in such place. I had the privilege of serving a tour of duty as captain of the head aboard the *USS Jacob Jones*, but not while Philbert was there.)

Cats have been part of the maritime community for years and years. In the olden days of wooden ships, cats were the effective enemy of shipboard rats, but cats are seldom seen aboard steel-hulled ships, especially naval vessels. I never saw any rodents aboard the *USS Jacob Jones*, so Philbert really didn't have to work for his room and board aboard the destroyer.

U.S. Navy ships sometimes have encountered rats, however. I recall hearing a story about a young naval officer who used cats to get rid of rats that had infiltrated his overage cruiser brought back into service during World War I. He sent a cat press gang into the neighboring cities of Norfolk and Portsmouth, Virginia. (A press gang was once a military detachment empowered to force men into naval service.) The cat kidnappers returned to the ship with a great variety of stray cats, some of them lean and mean characters. When let loose on the rat-infested ship, the ensuing battle was swift and unequal. The cats triumphed, and the young naval officer received a "well done" from his superiors for his rat-exterminating efficiency.

Philbert was a boatswain's mate first class. It said so in his personnel record kept by the ship's yeoman. The record was complete with paw prints, identifying scars (gotten in fisticuffs with landlubber cats), promotion entries, and conduct and performance marks (he never got anything less than a 3.0 out of a possible 4.0 rating).

Philbert's favorite hangout was the ship's galley, where he was given special treatment by the cooks. He was the ship's official food taster. No one ever got sick eating the same food that Philbert did. Being a Navy cat, Philbert was not a finicky eater; at times he would even eat baked beans, although he turned away from the corn bread usually served with the beans.

When the ship was in port, most sailors were eager to go ashore on liberty, but Philbert, while he was free to roam, preferred to stay aboard. There were times when he would venture down the gangway ladder to the pier, but he would stay close, and, after making an inspection tour of the dock area, he would scamper back aboard.

Once, before I became a crew member, Philbert had gone ashore while the ship was in the Boston Navy Yard and had not returned when the ship was ready to leave port. The ship's departure was delayed for over an hour while crewmen searched the docks for the cat. The engineering officer concocted a temporary boiler problem in order to allow the sailors enough time to locate the cat. Sailors finally found him, dirty and scratched, after he had tangled with a tough alley cat. Philbert received Captain's Mast and was property punished for his misdeeds.

Whenever the ship was to get under way after the cat's Boston escapade, the executive officer wrote in the morning order book a command to "arrest Philbert" several hours before departure time. This order would often puzzle a new officer of the deck, who would collar every returning sailor to learn if he was the wanted Philbert. The arrest order meant placing the cat in his special brig, a cage in the crew's quarters, until the ship had moved away from the dock.

Philbert was also placed in the brig whenever we conducted gunnery practice, fire drills, and collision drills. He did not like the loud boom-booms and noises

*Philbert was the ship's official food taster.*

associated with these necessary Naval exercises.

Philadelphia is called the City of Brotherly Love, and, when the *USS Jacob Jones* arrived there in the summer of 1938, Philbert decided that he had enough of the sea. He wanted to become a landlubber and, without any fanfare, walked down the gangway ladder and disappeared among the friendly folks in Philadelphia.

I'm sure he ended up telling a lot of sea stories to his newfound Philadelphia feline friends.

# 3.
# Kitty and the Chickens

The landlady was a kind old woman, but she was annoyingly inquisitive. Nosy would be the more accurate description.

Her cat was nosy, also, but then cats are always nosy, so I could tolerate him snooping around the apartment my wife Dulcie and I rented in Arlington, Virginia, after I had been discharged from the U.S. Navy.

The apartment was on the second floor of a white frame house with brown trimmings, located in an idyllic setting of old homes, some with wide porches and swings, most surrounded by aged and majestic shade trees, all having well-kept lawns and gardens filled with flowers and vegetables. Our landlady's property had something extra—a chicken house and a fenced chicken yard occupied by a couple dozens hens and a brightly colored rooster.

When we arrived to look over the apartment, the short and stocky landlady, dressed in a long gray dress with a black shawl draped over her shoulders, making her look older than she was, met us at the front door and ushered us into her parlor, where she introduced us to her husband, a tall, handsome gentleman, and her pet, a gray male cat named Kitty.

The old woman did all the talking, asking a lot of questions about our personal affairs and behaviors, obtaining our pledge not to throw any wild parties, not to play the radio too loudly or too late, or to walk too much or too heavily on the squeaky floor above her bedroom, or to drag chairs across the floors; but it would be all right with her if we bought rugs to cover the floors. We also agreed to wrap leftover food in newspapers and place it neatly in the garbage can so she could examine it to see if there was anything that could be fed to the chickens. And we certainly would not lean on the bannister of the staircase leading up to the apartment.

Despite these restrictions, we considered ourselves fortunate to find a reasonably priced apartment, because housing was scarce in the Washington, D.C., and neighboring Virginia and Maryland areas during the post-World War II years. Besides that, the apartment was located within a short walking distance to grocery stores, drugstores and the bus stop.

Kitty turned out to be a friendly prying cat. As soon as our furniture was delivered from the storage warehouse, the cat came up to the apartment and examined every piece of furniture and the content of every cardboard box. He trotted alongside me as I carried and placed furniture and knickknacks according to my wife's instruction. When I almost lost my balance trying to avoid stepping on the cat while carrying the bedroom mirror, I angrily barked, "Damn you, cat, beat it!" And he did.

*Kitty, the nosy cat who lived with our nosy landlady in Arlington, Virginia.*

Hours later, after we had returned from the drugstore with sandwiches and milk shakes (the refrigerator was empty), the landlady came to inquire about the cat. She had just finished feeding and watering her flock of hens and realized that she had not seen the cat for some time. Perhaps we had seen him?

Yes, we had seen him some time ago when we were placing our furniture, but then he disappeared. I did not mention that I had ordered the cat off the premises.

"He usually stays close to me at all times," the landlady said. She sounded worried. "It's not like him to go off for a long time. Maybe he became upset about you moving into the apartment. You know cats don't like any disturbances."

Should we feel guilty because her cat was missing? We volunteered to search for her straying feline and started our search in the kitchen, with the landlady trailing behind. As we moved from room to room, closet to closet, the landlady made comments about almost every piece of furniture, usually ending with the question "Did it cost much?" or with the declaration "I could use something like that."

The landlady became alarmed when she spotted my portable Underwood typwriter.

"That's a typewriter!"

"Yes," I agreed. "The typewriter and I go together. I'm a writer."

"Oh, dear," she moaned. "Typewriters make such annoying sounds. I hope you are not going to upset me with this typing business."

I assured the landlady that I had a pad to deaden the sound of the typewriter and I would be certain not to type late at night, and I promised not to go rat-a-tat-tat on the typewriter over her bedroom or parlor or kitchen.

One corner of our living room was stacked with opened and unopened boxes, and several layers of books and magazines were strewn about the floor waiting to be stacked in our small bookcase. The landlady went over to inspect the boxes and made a discovery—her cat was sleeping on top of the tome, *The Complete Works of William Shakespeare*.

"Ah, there you are, Kitty," she exclaimed, and her cat responded by making a combination purr and meow sound. She picked up the cat and stroked it, but when she put in down on the floor the cat jumped back into the box.

When I suggested that Kitty liked Shakespeare, the landlady countered that the cat probably like the cardboard box, and wouldn't I want to let the cat have the box. Sure. So the cat got the box and I kept Shakespeare.

Our apartment in Arlington had a small screened porch adjacent to the kitchen. From it we could view the wooded neighborhood and the landlady's garden and chicken yard.

One day, after taking a break from my writing, I relaxed on the porch, only to be alarmed by seeing Kitty walking about the chicken yard.

Cats and chickens don't mix, I reasoned, and, sensing imminent danger to the flock of fowls, I bolted down the stairs, dashed out the front door, and hightailed it to the chicken yard, all the while clapping my hands and yelling at the cat.

The startled cat stood its ground for a moment then, realizing that I was acting like a madman, decided that it was best to get out of harm's way. Meanwhile, the henhouse inhabitants, whose lives I was attempting to save, appeared to be more afraid of me than the intruding cat. In unison, the chickens cackled and chattered noisily while jumping about the henhouse and running around in their yard.

The landlady, hearing all the commotion, came out to investigate. When I explained that I was trying to save the chickens from certain death by her cat, she shocked me by breaking into a hearty laugh.

"Don't worry about the cat and the chickens. They get along fine," she assured me, but I remained puzzled and skeptical. How could she act so indifferent about the safety of her flock of hens? Wasn't the cat a predator?

A few days later I was to witness a scene that would remove my doubts about the danger of the hens mingling with the cat. There, in the middle of the chicken yard, stood the landlady with her Kitty beside her, throwing feed about for her flock of hens. The chickens came running and began pecking at the food, seemingly unconcerned about the presence of the cat. The landlady placed a dish of food on the ground, and, to my amazement,

*Kitty dined with (not on) the chickens.*

the rooster joined the cat to eat from the dish. What a wondrous sight!

The indifference of the landlady's cat to the hens was puzzling. Normally cats are quick to chase after birds, but to Kitty there seemed to be nothing bird-like about the chickens. Come to think of it, my cat Sonja in Norway did not chase chickens. Whenever Sonja was near the chicken yard she would stop and stare at the hens, then walk away, apparently reasoning that the cackling hens were some strange creatures not worthy of associating with.

It seems strange that cats and chickens could co-exist without any animosity toward each other. Certainly they were getting along better than many human beings.

# 4.

# Filbert, a Birthday Present

Dulcie acted coyly when I came home from the office that particular October day in the early 1950s. Perhaps she had prepared something special, like a sumptuous dinner or a surprise party; it was, after all, my birthday and a special one at that, my first birthday in our first home in Silver Spring, Maryland, mortgaged with the aid of a VA loan.

After giving me the customary welcome-home kiss, Dulcie maneuvered me through the living room and into the kitchen to the door leading to the cellar steps.

"Look down into the cellar," she said.

"What is it?" I asked, conjuring up thoughts about a birthday present, but at the same time unable to comprehend the importance of whatever it was being located in the basement.

"Just look," she demanded.

I opened the door, switched on the light, and looked down the cellar stairs.

Something moved at the foot of the stairs.

"Meow," it said. Then it meowed again.

"Why, it's a cat! A little kitten!"

The black and white kitten moving about the bottom of the stairs meowed pitifully and loudly, resentful of having been relegated to the loneliness of a darkened basement. While older cats will sometimes display aloofness around humans, even those who feed and care for them, most kittens are not skittish when it comes to establishing friendship. This kitten was eager for human companionship; as soon as I started to walk down to the basement, it scampered up the steps, meeting me half-way.

I picked it up and cradled it in my arms. The kitten was mostly white, but with a distinctive black spot on the head, like a skullcap, running from the top the eyes (with a slight dip below the left eye) to the back of its neck. The tail was black, except for the very end, which was white, as if it been dipped in a saucer of cream.

While I cradled the kitten, we both stared intently at each other as if we were silently asking, "Well, who are you?" The kitten stretched out one front paw and touched my chin. I responded by rubbing its belly, and the kitten reacted by wiggling its body and kicking its hind legs while pawing vigorously at my shirt. I released it promptly to let it explore the confines of the kitchen.

I was both pleased and surprised to see the kitten in our home. I was also puzzled because Dulcie, whose family had a dog named Bootlegger when she was a teenager, wasn't exactly fond of cats. Although she had never been hurt by a cat, she was always afraid that she might be scratched by their sharp claws. Some of her hang-ups about cats probably stemmed from old wives' tales, such as the one that purports that a cat lying on a child's breast can suck the breath out of the youngster. Not true, of course; a cat resting atop a person merely does so because it likes the warmth and comfort of the person's body.

When I asked how come we had a cat, Dulcie explained that it was a gift from our neighbor Ann Lamb or, more accurately, a contribution by her son Stephen, who had found the kitten on a grocery store's parking lot. Unbeknownst to Ann, Stephen had hidden the kitten among the groceries and her other children crowded in the back seat of the family car.

Stephen's capture of the stray kitten taught him an early lesson in decision-making and responsibility. One of his uncles, who owned a pregnant Persian cat, had promised Stephen the pick of the litter, but Ann and her husband Earl ruled that there would be but one cat in the Lamb household. Stephen would have to decide whether to keep the cat he had found on the grocery store parking lot or accept his uncle's offer of a baby Persian cat. Did he want to own and take care of a stray short-haired alley cat, or did he want to possess a purebred long-haired cat with silky fur?

Stephen opted for the Persian cat.

But what to do with the stray alley cat? Take it back to the parking lot? Let it loose to fend for itself? It would surely die of fright, starve to death, or get run over by a car. What to do? Stephen was in a quandary.

His mother had the solution: Give it to Mister Foss; he likes cats. Ann recalled Dulcie telling her how I reminisced about my childhood in Norway and the cat Sonja which gave me so much pleasure.

Stephen placed the kitten in a cardboard box; his mother phoned Dulcie and asked her to come out the backyard fence, where she would be handed a birthday present for her husband.

Dulcie was not too enthusiastic when she learned that the cardboard box handed to her by Ann contained a live, wiggling cat with sharp claws.

"What am I to do with this?" my perplexed wife asked as she gingerly accepted the cat in the box.

"Put it in your basement and run like the dickens up the stairs," replied Ann.

Dulcie dutifully placed the box in the basement and hurried up the stairs to escape the poor kitten, which was probably a most confused and frightened critter. Within a matter of a few hours, it had strayed into a dangerous parking lot to be chased and abruptly grabbed by a young boy, pinched and squeezed by the grubby hands of screaming children in the back seat of a car, picked up again and stuffed into a cardboard box to be carried away and dumped into someone's darkened basement.

The kitten, having explored the kitchen thoroughly, including rubbing its body up against all table and chair legs and peeking into the trash can, decided that it was tired and stretched itself out in front of the refrigerator. Smart kitty; it sensed where the food was kept.

The kitten seemed to have made itself at home, so my wife and I agreed, although Dulcie was somewhat hesitant (the cat's paws looked menacing to her) to accept the Lamb's birthday present.

The kitten had to have a name; it just couldn't go around being called "Kitty." A body examination, during which the kitten wiggled and flailed its paws furiously, revealed that we were the owners of a male kitten.

There was no hesitation in selecting a name for our new pet. It would be named after Philbert, the ship's cat aboard my favorite Navy ship, the gallant "tincan" *USS Jacob Jones*. The old destroyer was sunk by a German U-boat while patrolling alone off the coast of New Jersey in February 1942. All except eleven men were killed in the tragedy. Few destroyers suffered heavier casualties in World War II. I had been transferred off the "Jakie" just a few months before the sinking, so I knew every member of the crew. Many were close friends; one, Thomas MacDonald, had been the best man at my wedding just a month before the Japanese attack on Pearl Harbor. How quaint it is to have both joyful and melancholy memories at the same time.

Although Dulcie was agreeable to naming the kitten after my favorite ship's cat, she thought the spelling of its name ought to be different. Why not spell its name F-I-L-B-E-R-T as in filbert, the nut? It would sound the same as Philbert. Good idea; besides, next to peanuts, filberts were my favorite type of nuts. Later I learned that the filbert nut was named after St. Philibert, a Frankish abbot whose feast day falls in the nutting season.

I'm certain that the matter of name spelling was of no concern to our new family member, who seemed so content with his new surroundings that he fell asleep in front of the refrigerator. The phrase "asleep like a kitten" aptly described the tranquil sleeping position of the snoozing cat.

The following week was to be a breaking-in period for the three of us, but first I went off to the supermarket to buy items necessary for the care and feeding of cats—a variety of cat foods, a litter box, and a five-pound bag of kitty litter (I soon got enough smarts to buy the 25-pound bags of kitty litter).

It was decided to let Filbert have supervised roaming privileges of the house, but he had to sleep in a cloth-covered cardboard box in the basement, where his litter box was also located. The cat accepted these living conditions without a negative meow.

Filbert was probably about six months old and therefore very playful when we adopted him, and his spirited activities created no end of problems for Dulcie, who had the main task of supervising the cat while I was at work. Since the young cat pawed at anything that moved, Dulcie had to move lickety-split to avoid having her legs jumped on and scratched by the energetic cat. When she walked down or up the basement stairway, Filbert usually managed to swat at her feet through the openings between the stair boards. Then there were the frustrating times when she would catch Filbert pawing at the curtains or using the sofa as a scratching post. We later shelled out money for a genuine cat scratching post, which Filbert promptly ignored.

What would really cause Dulcie to have conniptions was Filbert's tiptoeing amongst her precious crystals, knickknacks and other collectibles displayed on shelves and bookcases. He seemed to take delight in performing these balancing acts. Perhaps he was trying to show Dulcie how clever and agile he was, or maybe he was a big teaser, knowing that his every tantalizing move would irritate his mistress.

Whenever my wife spotted Filbert near her precious things, she would clap her hands and shoo him away by yelling, "No! No!" These maneuvers were usually enough to make the cat stop his ludicrous acts. If, however, she scolded him severely, Filbert would scamper away and hide and sulk under a bed or behind the sofa or under the desk in my office. When the sulking period was over—it usually didn't last more than an half hour—Filbert would slink back into the scene of activity and make his presence known by rubbing his back up against Dulcie's legs. This was his way of saying "I forgive you," and she would respond by touching or rubbing his head. So then everything would be okey-dokey between the two friendly adversaries until the next time Filbert decided to try another fast one.

As the cat grew older and Dulcie became more accustomed to feline behaviorism, the two became great friends. Filbert obediently followed her around the house and out into the garden, where he played hide and seek among the flowers. He was always on hand when

*A Maryland winter scene shows Dulcie posing with Filbert, who loved to play in the snow.*

food was prepared in the kitchen, knowing full well that he would receive special treats as the official food taster.

Filbert also helped Dulcie on laundry days; well, sort of. Our washing machine (it didn't have all the fancy push buttons with various spins, rinse and dry cycles as today's machines have) was located in the basement next to a large sink. Whenever Dulcie prepared to use the washer, Filbert would sit next to the spigot and watch in fascination as the water poured into the machine. At times he would gingerly place a paw under the running water and would take delight in having the water spray on top of the washing machine and onto the floor. When his water trick caused him to drench himself, he would retreat to the safety of the stairway steps, where he would wash and groom himself, intermittingly casting a stern look at the offending washing machine.

Filbert was free to explore the outdoors, and he took full advantage of the opportunity, checking out all the nooks and crannies in the neighborhood, chasing after squirrels and birds but never catching or hurting any of them. Fortunately, he did not get into any scraps with other cats, but he did make friends with an old gray cat that came to visit quite often. Their favorite meeting place was the back porch. I imagined that the older cat was telling the younger one about his life's experiences.

As I said, Filbert did chase birds, to no avail; however, one summer day the birds turned the tables and gave him quite a rough time. I had stepped out on the back porch when I noticed Filbert tiptoeing on top of the chain link fence that bordered our property. Although it was not unusual for Filbert to prance on top of the fence to show off his grace of balance and agility, this time he appeared to be in an agitated state, his body hunched close to the rail and his tail swishing spasmodically. Suddenly, from out of nowhere it seemed, two mockingbirds dove at the cat, nipping at his back as they flew out of his reach. The cat let out an angry meow while maintaining his balance on top of the fence. Soon the birds were back for another attack. It was like a scene right out of a war movie, in which fighter bombers come out of the sky to strafe enemy targets.

Movies! That's it! I'll capture this bird-cat fight on film. I dashed into the house to retrieve my loaded 8-mm movie camera, all the time hoping that the actors would be on the scene when I returned.

I was in luck. They were still at it. The two mockingbirds appeared to have the cat trapped between them on the fence rail. The mockingbird in front of Filbert taunted him, nervously pumping its tail while hopping up and down on the rail, while its partner, approaching Filbert from the rear, alternately made a clucking and buzzing sound. Suddenly the rear bird fluttered into the air and with a shriek dove at Filbert, plucking a hunk of hairs from his back and then landing safely on the neighbor's rooftop. The cat cried out in frustration and, having decided that two hostile mockingbirds were more than he could handle, jumped off the fence and scampered to safety under the back porch.

*Angry mocking birds attack Filbert.*

Filbert and the mockingbirds are gone now, but, thanks to my amateurish filming of the combat scene, I can watch movie reruns and with amusement see how a small but highly dexterous force (the mockingbirds) took on and defeated a larger and dangerous enemy (the cat).

On the advice of the veterinarian, we had Filbert neutered. The vet assured us that after the operation the cat would become more docile and be a homebody, which in turn would keep him out of cat fights, thus reducing the chances of him being injured and becoming diseased.

The cat was quite upset when we brought him home after the operation. I don't know if Filbert realized that we had caused him to lose his "manhood," but I know for sure that he did not appreciate having the knife put to him in the vet's operating room. As soon as he was released from the carrying case, he made a beeline for the basement, where he went into hiding.

After about an hour's wait—I assumed that was enough time for anyone to sulk, even a cat—Dulcie and I went down into the basement to console the altered cat. We called him, but he did not make an appearance and greet us with his customary "meow, meow." He was hiding and he had plenty of places and things and boxes into which he could disappear from sight. As we began moving chairs, boxes, lawn furniture, garden equipment, laundry baskets, old newspapers and magazines, and other whatnots around in order to flush out the secretive cat, I had the feeling that he was hunched somewhere in the basement, watching our every move, gleefully enjoying our frustrations, and getting a slight revenge for the distress we had caused him.

After what seemed like hours of searching and suffering sore shoulders and tired arms from moving and lifting almost every movable object in the basement, I stood up to stretch my aching back only to stare right into Filbert's eyes. There he was, hunched as I surmised, in a small space up between the basement joists where cobwebs and dust had collected, his glassy green eyes glaring at me with contempt. He shied away when I reached out for him, but since he had nowhere else to go, he reluctantly let me remove him from the cramped hiding place. I cradled him in my arms, wiped away the cobwebs from his whiskers, and made sweet talk to him. He loved the attention, and soon life was back to normal.

While the castration or spaying of cats is supposed to make them more docile and stay-at-homeish, Filbert remained just as active and playful as before. He also continued to roam outdoors, especially in the evening, usually stepping out after supper and returning in a couple of hours. This routine continued unchanged after we moved into another neighborhood. I had taught him to respond to my call—Pssh! Pssh! Pssh!—the special cat call I had learned from my Norwegian grandfather. Filbert was usually ready to come into the house after a couple hours of evening explorations, and if he wasn't in immediate sight when I opened the back door, he would appear shortly in response to my call.

The neutering of cats is an operation that benefits the pet owner more than the animal, because the cat supposedly loses its desire to roam and thus avoids getting into fights with aggressive felines and other animals. With a docile, homebody cat, its owner, according to reasonings offered by veterinarians, will possess a more healthy animal and thus reduce the cost of health care for the cat. Not counting the cost of the alteration procedure, of course.

There is a truly humane reason for neutering cats: To stop or slow down the proliferation of stray cats that inhabit our cities and countrysides. I read somewhere that there are almost sixty million cats living as household pets in the United States. That's a large number of cats. It's nice that so many cats are being cared for, but there are still many millions of stray cats running helter-skelter, trying to stay alive.

De-clawing is a cosmetic operation that also benefits the pet owner more than it does the cat. Cat owners have the claws removed because they don't want the animals to scratch their precious furniture. What they are doing is making the cats defenseless if they should get into fights with other cats.

Cats may not like or use the scratching post you selected for them, but they can be trained to limit their scratching to certain areas and objects. The cats I've been associated with usually found it agreeable to do their scratching on certain mats or rugs I set aside for them. But I must admit that, like children, cats sometimes become naughty and will claw at the forbidden sofa. Well, nobody's perfect, not even the snootiest cat (or person).

After three years of living in our starter home, the two-bedroom brick rancher became less spacious with the addition of new furniture, knickknacks and collectibles, books and book cases, and other things. A large, executive-type desk greatly reduced the space in the small bedroom I had appropriated for my office. There was no dining room, and the small kitchen had barely enough room to seat four persons at our sturdy but plain Sears and Roebuck maple table. Adding to the space problem was the constant collection of "stuff," both the needed and unneeded kind, which invariably ended up in the basement to be forgotten and to gather dust. The arrival of overnight visitors, albeit there were few of them, meant rearranging the living room furniture to allow space for them to sleep on the sofa bed.

Agreeing that we required more space in order to enjoy a more comfortable living, our quest for a better home took us to Beltsville, close to the U.S. Department of Agriculture's experimental station and a few miles away from the campus of the University of Maryland. The new house, also a rancher, had added features of a larger kitchen, a dining room, and three bedrooms, one of which became my office.

Filbert had been with us about a year when we decided to move to another home. He had grown from a playful kitten to a fine specimen of a healthy male house cat who had become a player in the daily sketches of our life. While he was relegated to sleeping in a well-padded beer box in the basement at night, he spent most of the day in our living quarters. He slept just about anywhere he wanted, but his favorite resting spot was the sofa. Whenever we parked ourselves on the sofa to watch television in the evenings, Filbert would go to sleep on my lap. Sometimes Dulcie would shoo him off my lap and use it as a pillow while she viewed the TV shows in a stretched-out position (which usually led to her going to sleep before the shows ended). This maneuver annoyed Filbert to no end, and he would cry a pitiful meow as he sat nearby and glared at us with contempt. But soon he would jump back up on the sofa and maneuver himself into a comfortable position up against our bodies. We were a close-knit trio. Filbert ate his meals in the kitchen as would any cat that had been properly brought up by doting humans. A chair by the kitchen window was his favorite platform for watching the mockingbirds and blue jays tease him as they flew about the pussy willow that grew alongside the back porch.

I wondered with some concern how Filbert would react to us moving out of our home and into a new house miles away from his familiar surroundings. I had long heard stories of the proverbial attachment of cats to their homes, and frankly I was a bit worried that Filbert would spook and run away and try to get back to his old haunts once we had settled in our new home in Beltsville.

There is a lot of mystique and fascination about how cats are able to find their way home from sometimes hundreds of miles away. Maybe they have a built-in radar system that senses the earth's magnetism and leads them home over unfamiliar territory.

Not too long ago I read a newspaper account about a woman's new cat that bolted from her arms and ran away when she entered the veterinarian's office. The skittish cat, which had lived in her home but a few days after being rescued from the SPCA, wasn't about to enter another strange place filled with hissing felines and yelping canines.

The frantic woman and the vet's staff workers searched the area in vain for the lost cat. The grieving woman was afraid that she would never see her new pet again. Then, lo and behold—three days later—who shows up at her front door but the missing cat! Although the vet's office was seven miles away, and although the cat had never ventured outdoors during the short time it had lived with its new mistress, it had somehow managed to travel over strange terrain back to its adopted home.

A woman once told me a story about two cats who had traveled nearly fifty miles to get back to their old neighborhood. They had been uprooted from their home of many years when their owner moved his household to another town. While the new house met all the needs of the human members of the household, the cats decided that they did not appreciate their new home. So they left.

The owner and his family searched everywhere in their new neighborhood for the cats. Notices, describing the missing felines, posted on the telephone poles brought no response. Children were asked to bring stray cats for identification, but none passed the muster. After a couple of weeks of fruitless searching, the owner gave up all hopes of ever seeing his animals again.

Weeks and weeks had gone by when one day the owner received a telephone call from a former neighbor, informing him that his cats had returned to their old homestead. While the cats were skinny and dirty, and their paws were raw from walking, they seemed to be contented with being back in familiar surroundings. Since the cats did not recognize the new people living in their old home, they took up residence with their former neighbor. This was a natural thing for them to do because, whenever their owner went away on vacation and left the cats behind, they were fed and looked after by the kind neighbor.

This story has a happy ending. The kind neighbor adopted the wandering cats so they could live out their lives in a happy and familiar environment.

If you think fifty miles was a long trek for two cats, how about four hundred miles traveled by a Russian cat? In a recent year, the Associated Press carried a story about a Moscow feline who managed to find her way home from Voronezh, four hundred miles south of Moscow. The story was first told in the newspaper *Komsomolskaya Pravda.*

A year earlier, Murka, a gray and white cat, had caught and killed its owner's canary. Since this was the second bird killed by Murka, the owner had the cat banished from his Moscow apartment. The cat was exiled to stay with his children's grandmother in Voronezh. Murka stayed at the grandmother's house for only two days before disappearing.

One year later, when the owner was on his way to work in Moscow, he spotted the cat on the fourth floor of their apartment building, dirty and hungry and minus part of her tail and injured ear. Murka was glad to be home and out of the cold. During her yearlong journey she not only found adventure, but also romance. She came home pregnant.

As we neared M-Day—Moving Day—our small home had been transformed into a storehouse of cardboard boxes filled with our belongings. Filbert, probably unaware of the reason for the boxes, seemed fascinated by all the packages. He explored each and every box, either hiding in or going to sleep in the empties or scratching on or leaping over filled and stacked boxes awaiting the arrival of the moving company van.

When the movers arrived, I placed Filbert in the bathroom and warned the men not to open the bathroom door, because "there's a live tiger in there," explaining that I didn't want the cat to get loose during the moving turmoil. Little did I realize that I spoke the truth about the live tiger. When all our furniture and goods had been placed in the van, and I went into the bathroom to get Filbert to put him in his carrying case, I did indeed find that I had a wild cat on my hands. He made an attempt to escape from the bathroom as soon as I opened the door, but I managed to grab him by the neck and push him back inside. He was angry and

*Filbert: "You're not going to close the door on me!"*

hissed and clawed at me as I forced him into the carrying case. The bathroom was full of bits and pieces of toilet paper that the upset cat had shredded with his sharp claws, and, to show his further contempt for the moving event, he had urinated in the bathtub, not in the litter box that we had provided for him. Suddenly I had a feeling of uneasiness about moving Filbert into another home.

There was no need to worry about the cat moving into the new and strange house, however. Amazingly, he accepted the new house and its surroundings almost immediately, except for one brief moment when he wandered into the neighbor's kitchen, running slightly amok when the woman tried to shoo him out of her house.

Cats have an insatiable curiosity about what is going on, what is being kept behind closed doors, or what the content is of boxes and shopping bags. As we settled into the routine of living in our new home, Filbert made it his duty to check out every square footage of each room and closet, including the new dishwasher which, after a cautious inspection, he decided was too complicated to get into. He also did not appreciate the noise generated by the dishwasher and left the kitchen whenever the unit was being used.

Filbert did not like loud noises. I suppose this is a natural trait of felines who have a keen sense of hearing. Thunder would drive Filbert up the wall, and he would hide under the bed until the thunder claps stopped. One summer day, he was caught outside when a sudden thunder storm developed. I opened the door leading to the carport, expecting him to scamper in out of the rain, but there was no cat in sight. I looked around the carport and peeked under the car but found no cat. Then I called him a few times, and, just as I was about to step back into the kitchen, I heard a faint meow. I called him again, and he responded with a muffled meow. I lifted the hood of the car and there was Filbert, wet and dirty, cowering on top of the engine. He was shivering with fright, and when I picked him up he dug his paws into my chest so hard that I had to use force to pry him loose to release him in the kitchen.

The bang bangs and the shrill sounds of exploding and whistling fireworks that celebrating people enjoy on the Fourth of July and on New Year's Eve were not appreciated by Filbert. Nor did he like the voices of certain people speaking or laughing loudly. At times he would become so irritated over certain sounds emitting from the television set that he would leave the room, meowing angrily as he walked away.

Although Filbert enjoyed watching hockey games on TV (he'd stand up against the screen and try to stop the puck with his paws), he would leave the room whenever we tuned in on "The Patti Page Show." We enjoyed her singing and entertainment, but Filbert did not seem to appreciate her singing. Perhaps he was offended by her hit song "How Much is That Doggie in the Window?" or perhaps it was because of her sometimes monotonic renditions of sad songs.

From time to time, Dulcie's parents, Terrell and Katie Daffer, would motor up to Beltsville to visit us from their home in Norfolk, Virginia. Mr. Daffer, a city fireman, was a quiet, gentle person, who went about doing his duties without any stir, always appreciating the serenity of family life. Mrs. Daffer, on the other hand, was a happy-go-lucky person, always wanting to have a good time. At the peak of her enjoyment, be it from a good joke or a funny television skit, she could become quite boisterous, emitting an infectious, loud laughter that would have others joining in her merriment. But Filbert, offended by the rambunctiousness created by my mother-in-law, would walk up to her, give her a swift slap on a leg with one of his front paws, and then hightail it out of the room. His action only created more laughter, causing him to stay longer in hiding until things had calmed down. Fortunately, the cat never had his claws protruding whenever he struck out at Mrs. Daffer, but his slap was an admonition to "keep it down."

When watching African nature movies, I have always been impressed by the magnificent and attention-getting roars of lions and tigers. The roars made by their relatives in zoos doesn't seem to have the same oomph, inasmuch they have no need to assert their aggressiveness. In all the years I have been associated with cats (small sizes, not lions and tigers), I have never heard any of them make a roaring sound. Of course, they make a lot of angry hisses and moaning meows, but you wouldn't expect a small cat to emit a powerful roar or even a loud groan.

I should never say never because, believe it or not, Filbert was the first cat that I heard make an honest-to-goodness roar. Well, maybe I should call it a growl.

Anyway, it came about this way:

One day I picked Filbert up, cuddled him in my arms, and walked around the living room making sweet talk to him. Cats, as you know, love attention, and Filbert (while at times he would act grumpy) would go limp in my arms whenever he was the object of physical attention. I walked over to the front door and raised him up to allow him to look out through the narrow peep glass installed in the door. Since this was the first time that he had had the opportunity to look out through the peep glass, he became quite curious and a bit agitated. His ears perked up, and he pressed his nose against the glass as if to get a better view of what was going on outside.

"What's out there, Filbert? Do you see something?" I asked in a hushed voice.

To my surprise he responded with a growl—a "grrrr"—like a deep, harsh purr. He growled a few more times and then scratched at the peep glass, wiggling his body as if demanding that I free him to let him get at whatever was annoying him.

When I released Filbert and opened the front door to allow him to chase the imaginary intruder, he just stood still and stared out for a moment, then turned around and walked away. "Well, there was nothing out there, so what's to get excited about."

A few days later, I picked up Filbert and allowed him again to look out the peep glass. "Do you see anybody out there?" I asked. As if responding to cue, Filbert growled, wiggled his body, and swished his tail. But when I let him down and opened the door, the cat just walked away. "You look, I'm through."

We went through this peeping and growling routine a few more times until Filbert decided that the exercise was pretty silly. "Why don't you let me sleep on your lap while you watch TV or read a book or something?"

While Filbert liked to sleep (did you ever see a cat that didn't like to snooze?) he could also be quite active, even aggressively so. From time to time, I would get down on my knees, wave my arms and hands at him, and challenge him to a boxing or sparring match. Receptive to the challenge, the cat would slink about like his ancestors in the wild approach their prey, then make a sudden thrust at me with a paw. I would try to tap him with my outstretched hands; he would parry the blows like a skillful boxer and retaliate quickly with jabbing paws. Most of these sparring matches were conducted according to our own Marquis of Queensberry rules, i.e., cats will not employ protruding sharp claws when engaging in fisticuffs with humans.

To begin with, my sparring matches with Filbert were conducted under a gentlemen's agreement: I won't hurt you if you don't hurt me. That reminded me of the sparring matches I had as a boy in Milton, Massachusetts. My buddy, Ben Graham, who owned two pairs of boxing gloves, and I would spar in the garage, acting as if we were headliners like Jack Dempsey and Gene Tunney. We always agreed that while we could make soft jabs, we weren't to throw any hard punches to the opponent's face. Things didn't always work out according to the rules, and, once a fellow had "inadvertently" slapped the other guy too hard in the puss, all rules went by the wayside, and we usually ended up whaling away until one sparring partner got the better end of the bargain. Come to think of it, seems like I suffered many nose bleeds in those days.

Like my boyhood sparring matches with Ben Graham, my fisticuffs with Filbert would usually end when one of the participants got hurt, and, in the case of my fights with Filbert, I was always the one who got hurt and threw in the towel first. When our sparring matches became too rough, or if I tormented him too long, Filbert ended the match by rising up on his hind legs and giving me a real whammo with his sharp claws, ripping my hand. The bleeding loser would then retreat to the medicine cabinet and apply iodine and Band-aid to the wound. My wife Dulcie could never figure out why I would be such a glutton for punishment. Neither could Filbert.

*Filbert waits for Santa Claus under his stocking hung over the fireplace in our home in Beltsville, Maryland.*

Cats do not like to do what you want them to do. Dulcie learned the truth of that statement when she purchased a harness and leash so that she could take Filbert for strolls around the neighborhood. Filbert did not take kindly to her idea. He knew something was amiss as soon as he saw me coming toward him with the harness and leash. (Dulcie was smart: "You put it on him; he might scratch me.")

We tried the harnessing operation in the kitchen, figuring that the cat couldn't get away from our clutches. Closing the doors to prevent the cat's escape was a mistake. He knew right away that we were up to something no good.

I got down on my knees and held Filbert tight between my legs while attempting to place the harness over his body. The cat bit at the harness and wiggled and bucked and wiggled and bucked some more in a futile attempt to get away. And he also scratched. Released when the harness was finally in place, the cat acted like he was having a fit while trying to rid himself of the unwanted leather gear. He kept backing up under the kitchen table and chairs, all the time twisting and turning, trying to shed himself of the harness.

More protest moves ensued when we took Filbert outside to let Dulcie practice walking him with the leash. At first he sat down and stubbornly refused to move when Dulcie tugged at the leash. She tugged some more, while encouraging him to go for a nice walk, but Filbert did just the opposite—he moved backward. Then he bit the leash, jumped up in the air, rolled over, and yanked the leash away from a frightened Dulcie.

That was it! "Remove the harness and leash," Dulcie commanded, and, although I suffered through the agony of de-harnessing the cat, I was glad to set him free.

Filbert kept giving us dirty looks for several days before he forgave us for the dumb harnessing and walking-the-cat idea. As for the harness and leash—well, it was sold some years later at a garage sale to a woman who thought it would be a perfect thing for walking her little pooch.

Filbert was a friendly cat. People liked him, and he enjoyed being petted and fussed over as long as one didn't become too boisterous. You recall that earlier I told of how he objected to the rambunctious behavior of my mother-in-law.

Filbert also had friends among his peers. Since he made daily excursions around our property and the neighborhood, he had made the acquaintance of other pets living in the area. He ignored a couple of small dogs, treating them as discarded curs, but he became palsy with several cats who often gathered for a bull session (cat session) on our carport.

One member of Filbert's inner circle of friends was Prince Charles, an aristocratic-looking, gray fluffy-haired cat who lived across the street. At first the two cats didn't get along too well, but after a few spats, during which Filbert displayed his best alley-cat fighting techniques, they agreed to become friends. Prince Charles began acting like a commoner cat, even answering when we called him Charlie instead of the hoity-toity royal name.

The family next door had a female cat aptly named Curiosity.

She was a bit shy and reserved and would approach

you in a slinking, cautious manner. Curiosity was inquisitive about what was going on in the neighborhood; every now and then she would leave home for a couple of days or so. When the family, which also harbored two boys and a girl, adopted another cat and a German Shepherd puppy, Curiosity decided that three animals and three kids was a crowd and left the premises for good. She probably had staked out another family more receptive to her finicky taste during her frequent travels.

The new feline on the block was a short-haired, totally black male kitten, which the neighbors' children predictably named Blackie. Like all youngsters, Blackie was eager to show off his friskiness in front of Filbert, chasing his own tail, hiding in and jumping out from behind bushes, or just running senselessly up and down the driveway. Filbert, who had long outgrown these silly kitten-like antics, just sat and watched the kitten from his favorite vantage spot on the carport. When Blackie wore himself out showing off, he usually came over and rested beside the older cat.

Filbert and Blackie became real palsy-walsy, with the older cat assuming a kind of protective guardianship over the newcomer. It was quite amusing to watch the two cats play together. Filbert would let Blackie play his heart out, but when Filbert called it quits, he'd stretch out one paw and gently touched the younger cat on the head as if to say "enough already." Sometimes, when the eager kitten wouldn't stop, Filbert would make an angry hiss. Blackie was quick to take the hint.

Filbert liked to explore the neighborhood gardens and the open field behind our property. The field eventually lost its rural characteristics to a construction project. Whenever Filbert roamed in the gardens, he would walk gingerly among the plants and smell the flowers. I don't know if any particular flowers were his favorite, but he couldn't pass up a trip through the gardens without smelling the flowers. Blackie often would join Filbert during these garden excursions, which often turned out to be humorous events for human onlookers.

Some of my dear readers may be old enough to remember entertainer Ted Lewis and his famous "Me and My Shadow" song and dance routine. Lewis, dressed in a white tuxedo with top hat and carrying a white cane, would sing and dance to a very catchy tune, while, in the background, a black-attired dancer, also swinging a black cane, would mimic Ted's every move. The audience loved each show-stopping performance, bringing down the house with their rousing applause.

Well, when Filbert and Blackie went into the fields, they sometimes put on their own "Me and My Shadow" exhibition. Filbert would lead the way, and Blackie trailed right behind him. When Filbert stopped, Blackie would stop. When Filbert started moving again, Blackie would do the same. Since Filbert was mostly white and Blackie was totally black, it appeared to onlookers that Blackie was Filbert's shadow. Their movements certainly reminded me of Ted Lewis's clever dance routine.

There were times when Filbert decided that he had enough of Blackie's trailing-behind foolishness; he would stop, turn around and glare at the younger cat. I imagined him saying, "Get lost, kid! Go on home!" This admonition usually didn't work because, once Filbert started moving through the field again, Blackie resumed his faithful follow-the-leader position. When Filbert got really annoyed at Blackie, he would turn around and bare his teeth and hiss at the younger cat, sometimes even slapping a paw at the annoying cat. While Blackie would take the hint and stop for awhile, he would soon resume trailing Filbert, but from a safe distance.

A strange cat made its presence known in the neighborhood one day. It was a male tabby, a tiger-looking cat, with both striped and blotched red markings on his body. He appeared near our carport and, with an outburst of a series of high-pitched meow meows, announced to the world: "Here I am, pay attention to me!"

His yelling got the desired results. The resident cats showed up en masse to greet the newcomer. They were all curious and appeared not to be resentful over the outsider entering their territory. Filbert, upon whose domain the new cat had stepped, led the welcoming committee by placing himself in a strategic position atop a grassy mound from which he could look down upon—and perhaps from which to pounce upon—the other cat, which was sitting respectfully at the bottom of the slope. Charlie surveyed the situation from a few feet behind Filbert, and Blackie, not certain what to do, cautiously peeked out from behind a bush.

It chanced that Dulcie and I were in the back yard when the red cat showed up, and we feared that we were about to witness a cat fight. Breaking up a cat fight is not the smartest thing to do; I can assure you of that. I tried it once when Filbert and Charlie tangled, and while I thought I did a noble thing by picking up Filbert, I ended up getting the worse end of the deal, suffering bites, cuts, scratches and humiliation.

Filbert approached the new cat slowly, stopped halfway down the slope, then sat motionless and stared at the newcomer. The stranger, sitting at the bottom of the slope, made himself more comfortable by shifting his body to a prone position. The two cats seemed to have accepted each other without any misgivings.

"Who's your new friend, Filbert?" I asked as I walked up to the new cat and touched its head. "Meow, meow," the stranger responded, purring loudly and raising his head for more attention.

The new cat, which we promptly named Red, was a friendly fellow, always eager to let us stroke him or pat his head, actions to which he responded with soft meows and long purrs. We suspected that he was a stray because his body was marked with scars from past cat fights. While most stray cats look lean and hungry, this fellow appeared well-fed, so we reasoned that he begged food from the workmen at the nearby construction sites. Still, he might belong to someone in the neighborhood. Even so, we gave him food, which he gobbled up in a hurry while Filbert watched with interest.

It is said that once you feed a stray cat it will befriend you and stay with you forever. Well, that's exactly what happened after we had given the welcoming morsels to Red. He showed up at our back door the next day and the next day after that, and when days became weeks we accepted the fact that another cat had become a member of the family.

Filbert had accepted Red as a family member long before Dulcie and I did, but with one important proviso— the new cat could not come into the house. Whenever we opened the back door to let Filbert into the kitchen, he would hiss and slap at Red if the other cat tried to enter the house. Red made no serious attempt to challenge Filbert's territorial rights, accepting his status as an outside cat.

To make life easier for Red, I obtained a large, strong cardboard box which I lined with old rags and towels and placed under the bay window which projected outward from the rear wall of the house. The bay window protruded out far enough to prevent the box from being rained on, allowing Red to have a dry spot to sleep and rest. Red watched me rig his new shelter and stepped into it as soon as I finished; he smelled and encircled the bedding a few times, then lay down to wash himself, all the time purring profusely. I imagined his gestures were a cat's way of saying "Thanks, I appreciate this."

While Filbert and Red became good buddies, and while Red enjoyed the companionship of Charlie and Blackie, he frequently would absent himself from the neighborhood for several days at a time. I had no idea where he went during these outings, but sometimes he returned in a miserable condition, looking much like the loser who had tangled with a larger and superior cat. I would then cleanse his wounds with a liberal amount of hydrogen peroxide solution (much to his resentment, I might add) and then apply whatever other anti-infective medicine that was available in our special cat medicine cabinet. Mother Nature was kind to Red; his wounds healed quickly, and he appeared not to have suffered serious health problems from his pugilistic escapades.

Red did not get into fights with the local cats—at least I wasn't aware of any scuffle among them—but one day he took on the neighbor's German Shepherd dog. It was a surprise attack. A surprise to the onlookers and certainly a surprise to the dog.

Red and Filbert were lolling about the grassy mound near the carport, enjoying a restful afternoon, when Blackie's house mate, the German Shepherd, showed up in our backyard. The dog, now outgrown his awkward puppy stage but still lacking social graces, began barking at the cats, all the while jumping from side to side and forth and back as if it were challenging the cats to a chase. Filbert retreated to the higher level of the carport,

*Red attacks neighbor's annoying dog.*

looking a bit annoyed at the dog's interruption of his quiet afternoon. Red, on the other hand, arose from his resting place, arched his back and swished his tail in a show of anger; the warning signs did not register with the dog, who kept barking and jumping like he had fits. Suddenly the dog's barks turned to frantic yelps as Red jumped on its back, digging his sharp teeth and claws into its skin, all the while emitting blood-curdling shrieks. The dog, obviously in pain, was running around in circles, yelping for mercy as Red, his claws still dug into the enemy's fur, was riding the German Shepherd as a rodeo cowboy rides a bucking bronco.

The cat and dog fight, if you can call it that, was over in a few moments when Red released his ripping claws from the victim's hide, with the terrified dog running like all get-out away from our back yard. If Red had been a cowboy and the dog a bronco, I'm sure that Red would have stayed in the saddle the necessary ten seconds required to be declared the bronco-busting winner.

The German Shepherd didn't venture into our back yard too often after its run-in with Red. I assumed that it had learned a greater respect for cats, because subsequently it acted more gently toward its house mate, pint-sized Blackie.

Whenever Dulcie and I drove down to Norfolk to visit her parents, we boarded Filbert with the veterinarian. I don't think any animal likes to visit or spend a weekend or more at the vet any more than human beings enjoy going to the doctor or dentist. While most vets are kind persons and have caring staffs, I am not aware of any animals that are eager to spend any time in the veterinarian's domain. I have seen cats and dogs bolt furiously from the hold of their master at the sight of the vet's office door, and, once inside, some of the frightened animals shook as if they were shivering from intense cold.

Filbert didn't like going to the vet either, and he always knew when that unpleasant time had arrived. The cat-carrying case was a dead give-away. Whenever he spotted the carrying case, he would go into hiding but, once caught, would put up a good struggle with lots of wiggling and scratching before being subdued and secured in the carrying case. After much tribulation, we smartened up and eased the carrying-case struggle by me holding Filbert in my arms and then quickly forcing him into the case which had been hidden from his sight. Even so, the cat managed several times to scratch my hands before I could close the lid. In retrospect, I don't blame the cat for protesting and scratching to avoid being cooped up in that uncomfortable carrying case. It's like being thrown into the hoosegow for no reason. Later we were to get a larger cage-type carrying case in which the animal could sit and stand up and watch what was going on from three sides.

When we first boarded Filbert, the veterinarian asked if there were any special foods that the cat might want to eat while under his care. When I expressed surprise over the question, the vet explained that some animals become so stressful over being locked up in a strange place that they refuse to eat. These animals would probably feel better if they were fed their favorite food, perhaps even prepared by their owners, rather than the pet food dished out by the vet.

Filbert was not too persnickety when it came to food, usually eating most cat foods plus various meats and fishes we shared with him from our table. He savored bits of pork that we would offer him from our plate, but we didn't let him have pork too often since I understood that this meat was a no-no for felines. Somebody told me that or I read about it in some cat care pamphlet. Filbert did like to eat sweet peas, but only those canned by the Del Monte Corporation. He acquired a taste for the Del Monte sweet peas when Dulcie placed a spoonful of them in his food dish in an attempt to get him to eat vegetables. To our surprise he ate the peas with great relish, but he turned his nose up on any other kinds of vegetables.

As it turned out, Filbert did not get any special foods while he was boarded with the veterinarian, and while he may have lost some sleep because of the crying cats and yelping dogs in nearby cages, his appetite did not appear to suffer during the incarceration.

Sometime after becoming accustomed to having Red as a regular hang-arounder we made another motor trip to Norfolk to spend the weekend with Dulcie's folks. Filbert would be placed in the care of the veterinarian during our absence, but what to do with Red? We really didn't own him—he wasn't our cat—but since we had befriended him and as he showed up regularly for food, we now felt responsible for his well-being.

We decided that Red, too, would be placed in the care of the vet. He probably wouldn't like it, being the free-roaming animal that he was, but he just had to put up with the inconvenience for about seventy-two hours. Since we had only one cat-carrying case, I deposited Filbert first with the vet, then came back home to pick up Red; but by then the little tiger cat had decided that he had other plans for the weekend. We searched the neighborhood and called out for him, but Red was not to be found. Assuring ourselves that the cat had taken care of himself in the past and would probably do so again, we decided to get on our way, but not before obtaining a neighbor's promise that she would feed Red in our absence.

Our stay in Norfolk was pleasant, but we fretted over whether Red was safe, staying away from cat fights, getting his food and keeping warm because it was autumn, and the weather, especially at night, was getting colder.

I think our homeward journey was made in shorter time than previous trips. After having picked up Filbert from the vet, we approached our home with some anxiety and perhaps a feeling of guilt for having left Red behind to fend for himself.

As the car swung into the driveway, we spotted Red sitting on the carport, near the back door, as if waiting for someone to open it and let him in the house. He gave his usual high-pitched meows and, with his tail pointed skyward, walked directly toward the car. Rather than moving the car unto the carport, I stopped it on the driveway, fearing that I might run into the eager tiger cat. Everyone was happy to see each other; Red meowed, purred and rubbed us affectionally, and we in turn patted and stroked him, while examining him for any signs of him having been involved in cat fights over the weekend. Fortunately he looked healthy.

Meanwhile, Filbert was having conniptions over being ignored and being locked up in the carrying case. He growled angrily and jumped out quickly when I opened the case. To show his displeasure over being pent up, he relieved himself in the carrying case, but a good padding of old newspapers helped make the situation less messy.

The two cats met and appeared to have a conversation at the back door. I suppose Filbert told Red to mind his ways, that he was still the Number One Cat despite all the gushiness displayed by us over Red. When we opened the back door, Filbert rushed into the house, leaving Red sitting politely outside the door.

*Red and Filbert, a couple of lazy bones.*

Changes were in store for both cats. During trip home we had decided that, if we found Red alive and well, we would let him come inside, at least into the basement, during the nights. Autumn had set in, the nights were getting colder, soon winter and frosty weather would be upon us, and Red, who had now become our ward, should not be forced to suffer the hardships of being an outside cat. Our main concern about letting Red come in was the reaction of Filbert, who had been quite tenacious in his belligerent attitude toward Red whenever the tiger cat attempted to stick his head inside the back door. We feared being the instigators of a cat fight, and my past experiences had proved that it was not a good idea to get involved in such entanglements.

Nevertheless, we stuck by our decision and invited Red into the basement. I coached him toward the back steps leading down to the basement door, and he came quite eagerly, perhaps anticipating the big change that was about to take place. I opened the door slowly and found Filbert standing inside, alert as if to pounce upon a trespasser. I had a sudden feeling of trepidation as Red stepped inside the basement door. While Filbert had hissed at him and had slapped at him whenever Red had sought to enter the kitchen, he surprised me by letting Red enter the basement without any provocation. As Red walked around the basement inspecting its myriad cluttered objects, including his own litter box and his own bedding (a padded beer box), Filbert trailed behind him. When they stopped at several points, it appeared that Filbert was explaining to his house guest the mysteries about the various boxes and household and garden equipment sprawled throughout the basement. Red seemed impressed.

We were exceedingly happy over the turn of events. The decision to let Red come in, albeit only into the basement, was correct and met the approval of Filbert, and Red accepted it gratefully, although he continued his unscheduled, although less frequent, exploration trips.

There is a social hierarchy among chickens called pecking order. The top hen can peck all others without fear of retaliation; the second hen can peck the third hen, and so on down the line. I believe there must also be a sort of pecking order or dominance hierarchy among other animals, including cats. Whenever Filbert and his neighborhood friends—Prince Charles, Blackie and Curiosity—assembled on the carport, Filbert always appeared to be in charge. For whatever reason, perhaps simply because it was *his* carport, Filbert assumed the position of the Number One Cat. When Red first showed up, he too was relegated to an inferior social position, although he displayed enough battle scars to command respect and fear among most urban felines.

Now that Red had taken up residence in the basement, Filbert gave further evidence of unflinching control over his domain. Whenever the two cats sat on the stairway leading up to the kitchen, Filbert would always position himself on a rung higher than where Red sat. And when Filbert entered the kitchen, he would turn around and glare at and sometimes hiss and slap at Red, admonishing him to stay in his assigned place. It was kind of sad to see Red being so demeaned by Filbert, but Red accepted his secondary cat citizenship without rancor.

Cats are supposed to be mousers; that is, they are supposed to catch mice. There surely were mice living in our neighborhood, because there were plenty of wood piles and other junky places for them to exist in, but I had never seen mice captured by our clan of cats. I came to believe that our cats were too well-fed and/or too lazy to be bothered with such mundane work as mouse hunting.

Well, wait long enough and things will happen, and sure enough, one day, out of the blue, Filbert, with Red trailing right behind him, came racing up to the back door with a small field mouse wiggling in his mouth. As I opened the door slightly to get a better look and praise him for his triumphant hunt, the mouse escaped from Filbert's grip and dashed into the kitchen.

What a commotion that caused! Dulcie, standing by the kitchen sink, grabbed the weapon nearest her, a wet dish rag, and began swatting at the bewildered mouse, all the time yelling, "Get that thing out of here!" Meanwhile, I opened the back door wider so the mouse could be shooed out of the house. Filbert and Red, both eager to catch the escapee, ran into the kitchen, jumping wildly around the kitchen floor and darting around chair legs, but they failed to catch their prey, who cleverly eluded its pursuers when it spotted the basement door slightly ajar.

The mouse sped down the basement stairway with the two cats in hot pursuit. They braked suddenly at the middle of the stairway when they realized that they had lost the mouse. The clever little rodent had eluded his enemies by hiding in the basement joists. The cats looked confused and, I suppose, somewhat ashamed for having let the little critter make them look so foolish.

I closed the door and let the cats stay in the basement, hoping that they might search for and find the missing mouse. When I opened the door several hours later, I found the two cats sleeping contentedly on the stairway, with Filbert on a higher step than Red. Mousers they were not.

Filbert had been with us nearly ten years when we lost him. His was the most tragic of deaths; he had been poisoned by some cruel human beast who had caused similar deaths among other neighborhood felines. Fortunately, Filbert's contemporaries were spared that horror before the killing stopped. Unfortunately, the killer was never discovered.

Filbert was a faithful and loving cat. While he could be stubborn at times, and while he would become angry with me if I teased him too much, he would always end his capers with a display of love and affection.

One meets many people in one's lifetime, but few can be counted as true friends. Filbert wasn't a human being, but he was a true and loyal friend.

# 5.

# Red Becomes An Inside Cat

Red was away from home when Filbert died. Perhaps he was exploring among the new houses being built in the neighborhood, renewing acquaintances with the carpenters and bricklayers who had shared their lunch with him before we began feeding him regularly. Since Red had lived the rough life of an outside cat, one might expect him to be bit skittish and stay clear of strangers, be they animals or humans. But Red didn't seem to be wary of anything or anybody. He was a very friendly cat. He had a very engaging personality (yes, cats do have personality); people took to him almost instantly wherever he showed up in the neighborhood. I venture to say that Red probably knew more people and had more human friends that any other mammal living in the town of Beltsville. I suppose that his trust in others and his eagerness to join the crowd is what got him into trouble and fights with other cats who didn't want an intruder in their territory.

Red did not hesitate when Dulcie opened the back door and invited him into the kitchen after he returned from his latest sojourn in the neighborhood. He walked to the middle of the kitchen floor, stopped and looked around as if to see if he was being followed, perhaps by Filbert. Dulcie assured him that everything was all right by talking to him and patting him on the head, and he responded by emitting his high-pitched meows, purring and snorting at the same time. Red turned out to be a very affectionate cat. Whenever he was doted over, he would get quite excited, snorting, sneezing, drooling and purring, all at the same time.

Having assured himself that he was on safe grounds, Red stepped into the doorway leading to the dining room. Curious as to what lay ahead, he peered cautiously around the corner, stretching his neck and squinting his eyes, his tail vibrating nervously. When he finally made his move he walked with resolute steps, his body swaying from side to side like that of a tiger prancing through the jungle brush, all the time casting an inquisitive look at every piece of furniture he passed during his inspection tour of the dining room, living room and bedrooms. The layout must not have impressed him too much, because he trotted quickly back to the kitchen, where he made himself comfortable while Dulcie prepared him a dish of cat food and a saucer of milk. As he ate his food, he meticulously licked up the few morsels he spilled on the floor, stopping every now and then to look at Dulcie, indicating that he appreciated the food and the service. When he finished eating he flopped down on the scatter rug by the kitchen sink, stretched his legs, then curled up into the familiar feline snoozing position. Yessirie—I'm gonna like this, Red said to himself, as he fell asleep in the warm kitchen.

Now that Red had become an inside cat and we had assumed full responsibility for his welfare, we took him to the veterinarian for a physical examination and neutering. After careful examination, the vet determined that Red was in good health despite the fact that he had probably been scrounging for himself for an unknown number of years. Also, the many scars on his head, body and legs, mementos of past fights with cats and other animals, indicated that he may also have divested himself of some of those proverbial nine lives that cats are supposed to have. The veterinarian nicknamed Red the "old warrior," and said that our little tiger cat was the most good-natured feline he had had as a patient in a long time.

Where did that myth about a cat having nine lives come from, anyway? As a child, first fascinated with the purported mystic qualities of cats, I firmly believed that a cat possessed nine lives. Grown-ups told me that, so it must have been true. Well, it turns out that the old notion concerning the nine lives of cats goes back

*Red, then an outside cat, gets a hand-
out at our Beltsville home as Terri,
Dulcie's niece, watches.*

to ancient Egypt. Seems that the Egyptians had a cat-headed goddess, Pasht, who was said to have nine lives. The cat-headed goddess must have impressed a great number of people, because the belief that a cat has nine lives persisted and was accepted as truth through the ages. Even today there are many who believe that the cat has nine lives. Their belief may be bolstered by stories of agile cats surviving falls from very high places. A cat has a unique leverage mechanism in its limbs, giving it the rare ability to right itself in air during a fall and land upright, a characteristic which further strengthens the notion that a cat has nine lives. In reality, however, a cat lives, on the average, to fourteen years of age; but claims have been made of some cats living past thirty years.

Red may have been a gentle cat, but he was a regular loudmouth as he vented his frustration over being cooped up in a room or in the basement too long, or if we were too slow to open the door to let him into the kitchen after he had made his regular inspection of the neighborhood. When so aggravated, he would let loose a steady stream of high-pitched meow meows, which were certain to draw the attention of anyone within hearing distance. When he came home from his first visit to the vet, he jumped out of the carrying case and pranced up and down the street yelling to high heaven: "Meow! Meow! Meow! Hey, I'm back! Meow! Pay attention to me! Meow! Here I am! Hello! Meow! Meow!"

Red didn't get a chance to develop a pattern of living in our Beltsville home, because a few months after he had come in from the outside we pulled up stakes and moved to Virginia. I had become disenchanted with working in Washington, D.C., once a charming southern city but now transformed into a noisy vulgar metropolis with increased crime and traffic jams. I wanted to try something new, and Dulcie longed to get back to her home town Norfolk so she could be close to her parents, who were now getting on in years. It was spring 1967, and spring is the time to plant seed for new adventures.

Moving away from Beltsville became a hectic event. When my new bosses in Hampton wanted me on the new job in two weeks, it left Dulcie with the unglamorous chore of stashing all our worldly goods into the oversized cardboard boxes provided by the moving company, plus the nerve-racking task of showing the house to potential buyers and working out details with the real estate agent. Since Red had not been an inside cat long enough to establish a regimen of indoor living, the hustle and bustle involved in our moving did not upset him as it did Filbert when we moved from Silver Spring to Beltsville. As a matter of fact, he took delight in inspecting the boxes and their contents, some of which he appropriated as sleeping quarters.

Red took up temporary residence with the veterinarian the day before the moving van came to take our goods and place them in storage. We had arranged to stay with Dulcie's folks until we could find a new home.

While I had qualms about taking a cat for a long automobile ride, the vet assured me that the tranquilizer he had given Red would keep him calm during our trip from Beltsville to Norfolk. The vet was right, because Red behaved like the perfect gentlecat during the entire trip. He alternately sat up viewing the scenery and passing traffic, and slept or just rested on a large bath towel Dulcie had placed on the front seat of the car. In addition to being calmed by the tranquilizer, we reassured him (and ourselves as well) by petting him and sweet-talking to him as we progressed down the road. A litter box was handy, but, to my amazement, he did not use it until the end of the ride.

Upon our arrival in Norfolk, the Daffer's small home suddenly became smaller and more crowded with the addition of the suitcases, boxes, clothes, typewriters, books, and plants we emptied from our jam-packed car. For a few days, Dulcie and I drove around in every which direction checking out homes for sale, but upon seeing the futility of this effort—I was on unfamiliar grounds and Dulcie was a stranger in her home town—we engaged a real estate agent, a very competent once at that, who, after listening closely to Dulcie's wants and needs (it's the woman who makes the house a home), steered us to a lovely ranch home in a very desirable neighborhood in Virginia Beach. Within two weeks we had repacked the car, thanked the Daffers for putting up with us and Red, and moved into our new home.

Katie Daffer was more than happy to see Red leave her home; I suspect she was a bit intimidated by the cat. While she welcomed us with bear hugs and hearty laughter, she took a dim view of Red's presence in her kitchen and especially in her sitting room. The small room, crowded by too much furniture, including a large television cabinet and a love seat, was Mrs. Daffer's favorite hangout. It was also the home of Goldie, a yellow parakeet who viewed the scenery from a hanging bird cage. When Red first spotted Goldie, he surveyed the bird with a baleful eye; but after he realized that the bird was well out of his reach he lost interest in the parakeet. Instead, he concentrated on Mrs. Daffer's love seat. This would be his favorite sleeping place.

His decision did not set well with Katie Daffer. The love seat was her favorite piece of furniture. It was from the love seat that she watched her favorite television programs, the soap operas, and the news as presented by that nice man Walter Cronkite. The love seat was also the catchall for the boxes and bags she brought home from her shopping sprees, and it was a storage bin for the weekly collection of newspapers. It was from the love seat that my mother-in-law conducted such important business as clipping cents-off coupons from newspapers and magazines, reading her daily mail, making prolonged telephone calls to her friends and family, and sorting and resorting her massive collections of family photographs and seasonal greeting cards. So you can readily understand why she took umbrage at Red's takeover of her center of activities.

Yet, while she complained that "that cat has taken my place again," or that "he's crowding me," her actions belied her complaints. Mrs. Daffer was loath to shoo Red away. If Dulcie and I nudged Red off the love seat, Mrs. Daffer would remain silent and shift her position to make room for him when he returned to the love seat. Red loved attention and would purr loudly and emit a snorting sound whenever he was stroked, but he was not a playful cat who needed toys for amusement. He was perfectly satisfied just to be left alone to do his sleeping and resting on something comfortable, such as a cozy love seat. The fact that he minded his manners and caused no upsets, such as shuffling her coupons and pictures, probably contributed to Katie Daffer's reluctant acceptance of Red.

Red arrived at our Virginia Beach home after all the furniture had been placed in its proper place, at least for a few months until Dulcie exercised her penchant for rearranging furniture, especially the pieces located in the family room and living room. Since Red had selected the studio couch in the family room as his bed, he was pleased that Dulcie chose not to move it about too often. Some cats can be quite persnickety about what types of bed they want or where their beds are to be, but Red decided that the studio couch would be his bed as soon as he spotted it. Dulcie provided him with a large bath towel, which was okay with him because cats like to have clean, soft material to curl up on when they rest or sleep.

Although the studio couch may have been the spot in the house reserved exclusively as a sleeping place for Red, he would often sneak out of the kitchen-family room area and go into the living room, where he'd curl up on a cozy, overstuffed chair. The living room was off limits to Red because there we had assembled our better furniture and Dulcie's treasured collection of fine crystals. Whenever Dulcie found the errant cat in the chair, she would scold him gently: "Now, Red, you know you're not to be on that chair." The cat, knowing well that he had made a no-no, would utter a faint, whining meow, arise from the chair, and then walk slowly into the family room or kitchen, as if to savor every waning moment of his escapade.

I have often heard people say that they don't like cats because they are characteristically independent of humans. There are people who hate cats because they are terrified of them, and there are those who can't stand cats because they are allergic to fine hairs. Then there are people who generally scoff at the idea of any friendship between man and beast. What a pity. These people should be reminded of what Mark Twain once said in the defense of the cat: "If man could be crossed with a cat, it would improve the man, but it would deteriorate the cat."

Cats may at times appear not to acknowledge their human masters, and although they certainly don't subjugate themselves to the control of man as dogs do, cats are very receptive to human love and will respond with their own tender movements. Take Red, for instance.

Having lived outside and having fended for himself an untold number of years (he may have been abandoned and/or mistreated by his former owners), Red quickly accepted his new surroundings and the comforts of a people-oriented home. Once he became accustomed to inside living, he showed no desire to step outside, not even to smell the grass or the flowers. While he liked to roam around the basement of our Beltsville home, he absolutely refused to enter the garage of our new home in Virginia Beach. (Most houses in the tidewater region of Virginia don't have basements—too close to the sea level.)

Red liked to be petted and talked to (even human beings enjoy such pamperings), and he responded in kind, usually by purring loudly and emitting his unusual nervous snorts, stretching his legs and clamping and releasing his front paws as if he were kneading bread dough. And, as most cats do when they respond to tender pets and strokes on their backs, Red would stick up his tail and elevate his rear end in a beautiful display

*Dulcie and Red take a cat nap.*

of cat body language, meaning "I love you, too."

Red was not a playful cat, but he liked to be dressed up. This needs a little explaining. When he parked himself on the studio couch, Dulcie would prepare a clean bath towel for him to lie on. At times she would place another towel over him, completely covering him from head to tail. Then one day Dulcie placed a colorful silk scarf over him, and when Red rose up after his nap the cloth draped over his head and shoulders in the fashion of a woman wearing a scarf. It was an amusing sight, and from then on Dulcie would often dress Red with the scarf. He was a willing participant in her dress-up game. When he viewed the backyard scenery—the trees, flowers and birds—through the glass door, sitting on his favorite seat, a lid-covered wooden bucket, and decked out in the scarf, he looked like a small peasant lady.

Red made no protests when we placed small paper hats on his head. Most cats would have tried to rid themselves of such attire, but Red was quite passive, as if it were the proper thing for cats to wear those silly head coverings.

Life is full of routines—modes of behaviors. We develop them and fall into them in our association with people at the work place, with businesses, and, of course, in our home. We develop certain routines with our family members, neighbors, and yes, even with our animals. There was one routine that Red and Dulcie practiced together. After supper Red would appear in the kitchen and patiently wait for the dishes to be washed, wiped and put away. Then he and Dulcie would retire to the master bedroom, where they would lie down on the bed and take a well-deserved nap. (I often wondered: Did Dulcie take a cat nap and Red a people nap, or was it the other way around?) Amazingly, while he had every opportunity to do so, Red never sneaked uninvited into the master bedroom. At times, when I worked late in my office, Dulcie would take Red and retire to the bedroom to watch television. Soon the sound from the TV set would act like soothing syrup, and both Dulcie and Red would fall asleep. When it was my turn to go to bed, Red would mildly protest my picking him up and placing him on the couch. He'd usually glare at me—a dirty look, it was—and grunt a short, moaning meow of disgust.

Whereas Filbert had enjoyed hanging around my office, checking out the book cases, trying to figure out how to remove papers from open file cabinets, and burying himself under a pile of newspapers and magazines, Red showed little interest in my office, except to take cat naps in a cushioned wicker basket we had provided for him.

The years of suffering through the hardships of outside living had sapped much of the vitality of Red. The veterinarian in Maryland had warned us that Red, the "old warrior," was an aging cat. We noticed that he slowed in his movements and that he preferred sleeping and resting to exploring as healthy cats are wont to do. A veterinarian in Virginia Beach examined Red, found him to be an old, worn-out cat, and administered a necessary dose of medicine in hopes of perking up his appetite.

One evening when I was typing the finishing touches to a magazine manuscript, Red sauntered into the office and lay down in his wicker basket. As is the customary thing for cats to do, he kneaded the cushion with his front paws and shifted his position several times before he found the proper sleeping position. Finally, with his head resting on his front paws, Red fell asleep. Dulcie came into the room and covered him with the brightly colored green and yellow silk scarf. "That will make him sleep better," she said.

An hour or so later I finished typing the manuscript and reached down and gently stroked the sleeping cat. He did not respond to my affection. Red was in his final sleep.

The "old warrior" had gone to his Valhalla.

# 6.
# The Handpicked Cat
# and the Rejected Cat

Time, the healing process for overcoming the pain and sorrow of having lost someone you love, a family member, a close friend—in our case, Red—had run its course. So when Dulcie one day said, "We should get another cat," we agreed that we missed the charm, love and companionship offered by a cat.

It was not without some trepidation that we approached the SPCA in Virginia Beach. Since there are definite responsibilities in connection with the ownership of a pet, we had given serious thought to the kind of cat we would select. Naturally, we hoped that we would find and select a healthy cat, but we didn't want an older animal inasmuch it would probably be as set in its ways as we were in our mode of behavior. We were looking for a young animal, a cat that would be home-loving and affectionate, a cat that would be our friend and companion for the rest of its natural life. Whether to choose a male or female cat when selecting our new pet was of little importance at that time since we had already decided that the chosen cat would be altered after it had been properly examined by a veterinarian. Altered cats make excellent companions, are more home-loving, and less inclined to fight. Our new cat would be a homebody like us.

We were greeted warmly by volunteers of the SPCA (Society for the Prevention of Cruelty to Animals) and a sign on the door that announced "Loving Pets for Adoption." After explaining that we were in search of a young cat to fill the void left by Filbert and Red, we were led to a chicken-wired pen, where a slew of cats of all ages, shapes and sizes and colors, sat, meowed, slept, meowed, groomed themselves, meowed, ate, meowed, played, meowed, fought, meowed, and scratched and pawed at the chicken wire in attempts to free themselves from their Babel of catdom.

Most of the cats and the kittens in the pen were either strays or castaways, animals discarded by owners who had grown tired of them. Children who get kittens because "they're so cute" sometimes won't have anything to do with their pets once they grow up and lose their cuteness. Some people who move out of town think it's too bothersome to bring along their pets, so they leave the poor animals behind to struggle for themselves.

The cats and kittens in the pen were living on borrowed time. If no one would claim them or adopt them, most of the animals would be put to sleep—euthanized—in a few days. While the SPCA attempts to find new owners for all its animals, it must by necessity arrange to have the unlucky losers destroyed. The thought did not cross our minds at the time, but in a few minutes we would be making a life or death decision—selecting a cat to live that might otherwise have been destined to be exterminated.

There were about twenty or more cats and kittens in the pen and they all looked adorable, making it extremely difficult for our somewhat confused minds to focus on a single animal. A black kitten, meowing loudly and sticking its paws through the chicken wire, attracted our attention as we paced from one side of the pen to the other. It cried so loudly that one could look down its throat and see its vibrating vocal cords.

We had almost decided on selecting the eager black kitten when we became aware of a young gray and white cat sitting atop a box and staring at us. The cat projected a majestic pose, looking somewhat bored and aloof, detached from its surroundings and fellow felines. Without moving a muscle, its shiny yellowish eyes followed our every move. Its penetrating stare and the fact that the young cat had assumed an air of confidence in spite of its plight drew my immediate sympathetic approval. I had always liked and preferred the independent attitude and behavior of cats over other animals.

Dulcie and I agreed that we would adopt this cat

that displayed so much class and charm. As one, we pointed toward the cat and in unison called upon the SPCA attendant to bring it to us for a closer examination. The cat apparently anticipated our decision because it stood up, raised its gray tail skyward as a sign of approval, and allowed itself to be picked up and placed in my arms without any hesitation. It seemed quite relaxed and purred slightly as I stroked and cuddled it in my arms. As the young cat looked at me, I took particular notice of its unique facial feature, a prominent streak of gray hair running from the middle of the forehead down to the tip of the nose. It looked as if someone had finger painted its white face. I ran my finger down the gray streak of hair, and the cat reacted by grabbing my finger gently with its front paws. Stretching its paws upward to my shoulder, it dug its claws into the collar of my jacket and stayed anchored there until we got into the car.

Our first handpicked cat—the others had been dropped on or dropped in on us—turned out to be a young female domestic short-haired member of the Felix Catus genus, of unknown ancestry, of course, but acting like she was descended from royalty. Exercising her royal powers, she decided that the headrest of the driver's seat would be her throne. She must have been chauffeured before, because she acted perfectly calm and self-assured as we made the journey to her new home.

The first thing the young cat did when she arrived at her new home was to give the garage the once-over. Since we had lived in our house less than two years and the garage was relatively clean and empty of boxes and stuff, her inspection tour was short. In the future, however, as the garage filled up with lawn movers, tools, lawn furniture, more boxes and stuff, the cat would spend hours upon hours checking and double-checking every nook and cranny of our place of disarray. She would also take pleasure in checking out the car whenever it returned to the garage from having taken me to work or having ventured forth to the shopping malls or grocery stores for people vittles and cat food. Her favorite resting place in the garage was on top of the car, especially after it had been washed and waxed. When the cat was atop the car, she would strike a regal pose, as if she

*Sonja considered the top of the car her throne.*

were resting on her throne. Perhaps she was.

The young cat didn't waste any time in getting herself acquainted with her new home. She followed us dutifully from room to room, stopping every now and then to smell a certain chair or table or view with special interest the rows of books and pamphlets in the book cases (a literary cat, no doubt!) and finally making herself comfortable on the family room sofa.

Sitting on the sofa and stroking the lovable young cat, I became nostalgic and commented to Dulcie that the new cat reminded me of the first pet I had as a child in Norway. There's something special and wondrous about first events in your life—they are solidly etched in your memory bank—you'll never forget them, and you can recall them as vividly as if they happened yesterday.

Dulcie was familiar with my childhood cat stories, so I was pleasantly surprised when she suggested that we name our new cat Sonja, the same name as my first cat in Norway. The new cat wouldn't be named Sonja the Second, or Sonja II, or Sonja the American cat, but simply Sonja. We "discussed" with the new cat the matter of the name, and she seemed to approve of the name selection. Since the cat knew that she had been assured of a permanent home with plenty of food and love, it probably didn't matter to her what we called her, Sonja or just plain Cat or Queen Isabella. Come to think of it, she probably would have preferred being named Queen Isabella because, at times, as she grew older, she acted high and mighty like a snooty queen.

Sonja was the cuddliest and most adorable young cat and brought immediate warmth, pleasure and love into our home. Most cats that live with a family and are well treated respond in kind by being wholeheartedly affectionate; they are not at all the supercilious, unresponsive creatures that some people like to paint them.

Sonja loved to be petted and was particularly fond of having her soft belly stroked. During the belly-rubbing sessions she would stretch her legs and roll from side to side, sometimes emitting a soft purr, indicating with her beautiful body language that "I'm happy. Stroke me some more."

Sometimes, in her eagerness to display affection, Sonja would bite my hand or arm. These "love bites," while meant to be sort of cat "kisses," would at times be strong enough to draw blood. At first I scolded her for biting too hard, but as I became attuned to her quirkiness I ignored her bites and scratches, accepting them as imprints of affection in a cat and man relationship.

There are people who scoff at the idea of friendship between man and beast, but I have lived long enough to know that man and animals, even man and fowl, can strike up and endure lasting friendship. Humans who have seen fit to domesticate cats and dogs and other animals—to make them their pets or play things—have the responsibility to treat these animals with kindness, even to the point as declared in human's wedding vows—in sickness and in health until death do us part.

Cats are by nature clean animals. I noticed that our cats spent a great deal of the waking hours grooming themselves. A cat can be in a deep sleep, wake up and immediately proceed to wash itself, and in a few minutes later go back to dreamland. I am certain that if cats had been accustomed to the use of a mirror, they would probably spend hours upon hours primping themselves in front of it.

Dulcie appreciated the cleanliness of our cats. Since

the cats liked to sleep on clean bedding, she provided them with a supply of old (but clean) bath towels that were strategically placed on sofas and stuffed chairs. The cats usually slept in padded beer boxes, but in a moment of silliness we purchased a four-poster cat bed for Sonja. She slept in the fancy bed for some time but eventually gave it up in favor of her favorite beer box.

Sonja and I had one thing in common—we both enjoyed newspapers and magazines, but not for the same reasons, of course. As soon as Sonja saw me sitting on the sofa or chair reading a newspaper or magazine, she would jump upon my lap and make an effort to lie down on my reading material. Sometimes she would be satisfied if I allowed her to park herself on the portion of the newspaper I was not reading. However, at times she could be quite contrary, insisting that she be permitted to sit on or lie down on the particular paper or magazine I held in my hand. Veterinarians who know about these things say that, by sitting on these papers and magazines, Sonja was marking them with her odor—giving them her stamp of approval. Maybe so, but there were times when her antics irritated me, especially when I was typing my manuscripts.

Sonja hung out in my small office jammed with an old desk, a file cabinet, book cases, and a credenza which served as a combination table and file cabinet. Sonja used the credenza, located by the window, as a place to sleep and from which to watch the goings-on in the front yard and the street. She would also sleep on my desk, if she was so inclined, which she was quite often.

Sonja seemed to have an *nth* sense in knowing when I was typing the final copy of my manuscripts. After sitting for a while on the credenza watching intently the typewriter carriage move and listening to the clatter of the typewriter keys, she would jump over to the desk and park herself on top of the draft or finished manuscript pages.

Admonishing her that she was holding up the works, I would pick her up and place her back on the credenza. She would look annoyed, then lie down and stare at me as if she were pouting. A few minutes later she would jump back onto the desk, and I would agree

*Sonja, the literary cat, liked my papers and manuscripts.*

that she could stay if she behaved. To soothe her feelings I would let her lie on some sheets of clean paper, stroke her back and rub her belly. While it worked every time, I realize that it was the cat who won in the end.

Sonja was literary cat, no doubt, because most of the manuscripts she sat on and gave her approval to were accepted by receptive editors. Cat-loving writers of renown, such as Mark Twain, Charles Dickens, Henry James, Ernest Hemingway, Paul Gallico and Cleveland Amory, would appreciate having a nosy and lovable cat like Sonja around when penning their great works.

While driving to work one spring morning, I passed through the older section of our neighborhood where the lawns are well-kept and the homes are shadowed by large, graceful oak trees. Some of the properties rim a small lake and a narrow park that are usually filled with wild ducks, geese and sea gulls waiting for a handout from their human neighbors and visitors. A sign at the entrance to the community tells the visitors that this area is a bird sanctuary; traffic signs by the park and

*Castaway Thomas is confronted by angry ducks.*

lake encourage the motorists to drive slowly because of "duck crossing."

My quiet drive through this pleasant scenery was suddenly shattered by the roar of a car, which sped away as its driver threw a white object into the park area. I slowed my car and glanced toward the object. At first I thought the driver had tossed a bag of bread out to the waiting ducks, but to my surprise the white object moved!

Curious, I stopped the car and walked over to the park for a closer look. The object turned out to be a white kitten. The frightened creature cried pitifully as it tried to find a safe place to hide from me and the perturbed ducks. Several of the larger ducks approached the kitten with their necks outstretched in a menacing manner. Shooing the angry (perhaps they were only overly curious) ducks away, I picked up the squirming kitten and brought it into the car.

"Now, what kind of person would toss a cute little thing like you out into the cold, cruel world?" I asked the scared kitten. It replied with a series of high-pitched meows.

"Well, what am I doing to do with you?" I tried to comfort the wiggling castaway in my arms. Again it responded with more high-pitched meows.

One thing was certain. It was in fine voice.

After closing the car windows so the little animal couldn't escape or hurt itself, I drove back home; I awakened Dulcie, who had crawled back into bed after serving me breakfast, held the little kitten in my cupped hands, nudged its nose and whiskers up against Dulcie's face, and said, "Look what I found."

"Oh, isn't it cute!" was the first thing Dulcie said. The second thing she said was "What are we going to do with another cat?"

I reasoned that we wouldn't keep the kitten that the crude man had thrown away amongst the ducks, but would safeguard it until we could take it to the SPCA, from where it would end up in a nice home. To protect the kitten from the jaws and claws of Sonja, we decided to hide the white kitten in the guest bathroom. I would take it to the SPCA when I returned home from work.

My day, which had begun with the unexpected rescue of an unwanted kitten, ended with the unexpected announcement by Dulcie that we would adopt the little creature. "I always wanted a white cat," she explained.

It was an adorable kitten. Cute as a button, as the saying goes. Its ears appeared to be inordinately large, but this may have been an illusion because of the prominent pink of the ears. Its paws also had a hue of pink to them. What made this kitten most attractive was its brilliantly shiny blue eyes. They shone like the sunlit blue Mediterranean Sea. This kitten was truly different than other young cats.

It was also full of fleas.

The fleas made themselves known when I gave the kitten a cursory physical examination to see if it had any cuts or bruises from being manhandled by its former owner. The exam also revealed the kitten's gender—it was a male. A quick trip to the veterinarian resulted in a special dip that killed the dastardly fleas. The vet also pronounced the kitten to be a healthy animal.

Well, now, we already have a grown female cat. Is it safe to bring a second cat—a male kitten—into our home? Won't the older cat make mincemeat out of the young one?

The vet assured me that since our cats were of opposite

*Thomas grew from this ...*

*... to this.*

sex, and since both cats were neutered (the white kitten was "fixed" before he came home), they would not be a threat to each other. We should, however, be prepared for it to take at least two to three weeks for Sonja to accept the newcomer. The meeting between Sonja and the new cat, which we decided to name Thomas, took place in the family room, a most appropriate place for everybody to get together. Sonja was well aware that there was another cat in the house. She could hear Thomas yell and scratch while locked up in the guest bathroom.

When Dulcie opened the office door, Sonja bolted out and ran into the family room. She came to an abrupt halt when she saw me sitting on the sofa holding the new cat.

"Look Sonja! Meet your new friend."

I held the wiggling Thomas on the floor as Sonja approached him. She moved slowly toward him as if she were approaching a prey. Would she attack the kitten?

The two cats touched noses and instantly recoiled as if they had been stricken by a spark of electricity.

I released my grip on Thomas, and Sonja circled him inquisitively.

Who is this character? What's he doing here?

The young cat uttered a couple of loud meows and tried to follow Sonja, but then decided to sit while being scrutinized by the older cat.

After making several circles around Thomas, Sonja decided that the newcomer was harmless. She sniffed at him a few times and then walked to her food dish in the kitchen. Thomas dutifully followed her, eagerly gulping the soft canned food we had made available to him. In the future, Thomas would not tarry when it was feeding time.

After a week of keeping the two cats separated at night—Sonja in my office, Thomas in the guest bathroom—we let them get together without any human interference. They got along just fine, thank you. Sonja did assert her seniority and pushed Thomas aside whenever she wanted to be the center of attention. The younger cat made no effort to attract anyone's attention.

Thomas turned out to be a fraidy cat. I suppose his

timorous behavior stemmed from him being mistreated by his previous owner, or maybe, like some people, he was more shy and timid than other cats. Whenever anyone visited, Thomas would hide under a bed or table or behind the sofa. Sonja, on the other hand, would let her presence be known, rubbing her body up against visitors' legs and accepting their friendly gestures. Most cats love to be cuddled and stroked, but Thomas tolerated only a few moments of affection before abruptly scooting off as if saying "enough!"

While Thomas acted like a fraidy cat around strangers, he was most aggressive when it came to eating. Whenever Dulcie or I plunged the can opener into a can of cat food—or any other canned food for that matter—the cutting sound was a signal for Thomas to run into the kitchen. At times he would gallop, emitting short grunts as he approached his food dish.

Cats usually have discriminating appetites, eating only enough to satisfy their hunger. Thomas had a ravenous appetite, gulping the food down as fast as he could. At times he would even try to steal food from Sonja's dish. As a result of all this eating, Thomas grew so fast and became so big that he reminded me of a Norwegian folk tale about a gluttonous tabby that ate everything in sight and grew so much that she finally burst. Well, Thomas didn't burst, but he certainly was a heavyweight, at one time weighing in at over twenty pounds.

One of the reasons for Thomas' compulsive eating could have been the neglect he suffered as a kitten before he was abandoned by his previous owner. I once read an article by an animal doctor who said that cats, like people, often overeat because they feel anxious or insecure.

Whereas Thomas would eat whatever food was presented to him, Sonja was quite persnickety about the food she was given. She seldom ate all the food in her dish and often put her nose up in the air and walked away from strange foods. At times she would show her strong dislike for a new food by pawing over it in the same manner she would cover up a bowel movement in her litter box.

Sonja and Thomas became the best of friends. They ate together and slept together—well, that's not quite

*Two sleepy cats.*

true—they slept in the same room, my office, in separate beds. Sonja preferred sleeping in a beer box, but Thomas liked the large dog-type wicker bed we had gotten for him. Once, Dulcie opened the door to the office and found both cats cuddled together in the wicker bed. She thought their coziness would make a cute photograph, but when she returned with the camera Sonja had gotten back into her beer box. Dulcie admonished her for being "fresh," but Sonja just curled up and went to sleep.

When the sun shone through the office window, the cats would lie down on top of the credenza and enjoy the warmth of the sun rays. Sonja took up her post close to the window, relegating Thomas to stretch his long body on the credenza. When the weather permitted opening the window, Sonja stretched out in the window sill up against the screen. At times she would shift her position, lying on her back with feet stretched out, sleeping contently and looking like she was completely out of this world. Perhaps she was.

Cats that are allowed outdoors usually find a convenient tree or wooden post on which to stretch and claw. However, indoor cats like Sonja and Thomas develop a habit of flexing their claws on rugs and furniture, thereby upsetting their owners. We tried giving them a scratching pad and scratching post, but the two cats showed little interest in these items, except when Sonja decided to use the scratching pad as a bed. For a while we solved the scratching problem by putting down two old braided scatter rugs, one in the office and the other in the garage, but the cats still managed to scratch the sofa and upholstered chairs when we weren't looking. When caught in the act and yelled at to "stop it!" the cats either ran and hid or just stopped scratching, giving us the "I wasn't doing anything" look. Just like kids, cats will be cats.

The reason Sonja probably liked to lie down on top of the scratching pad was that it had been treated with catnip, but after the scent of catnip wore off she ignored the pad. While Sonja enjoyed the scent of catnip, Thomas wouldn't have anything to do with smelly stuff. He'd back off whenever we presented him with a catnip-scented toy.

Sometimes when I sat on the sofa reading or watching TV I would kick off my shoes to be more comfortable. Quite often, Sonja would then come to my side and start playing with my footwear. She'd bite at the shoe laces and push her paws into the shoes, ending her entertainment by poking her nose into the shoe and going to sleep. I wonder if Sonja enjoyed my shoes because my feet smelled. Like catnip?

Sonja and Thomas gave us much love and affection and enjoyment over the years, but, as it must to all living things, death took them away. Thomas died suddenly after a short illness; he was only about five years old. Sonja led a long life—14 years—and to the end she was as graceful, affectionate and responsive to our touch and love as she was the first day she came into our lives from the wired pen at the SPCA.

Dr. Doolittle talked to the animals and so do I. Talking to the animals can get you into a lot of trouble, I suppose, if the wrong person overhears your conversation. There is nothing "funny," however, about talking to the animals; farmers do it all the time, and most people think that's quite proper.

Talking to a cat is better than talking to yourself. Besides, I noticed that whenever I talked to a cat it would at least seem interested in what I was saying, which is more than I can say about some people I have conversed with. Sometimes the cat would get into the conversation by emitting a little meow, as though to agree to or remonstrate with my statements.

There are people who say that cats and other animals really don't understand a word you say to them, that they just react to the inflection of your voice, but I know better.

It was nice talking to you, Sonja and Thomas.

# 7.
# A Happy Ending

We have not owned a cat since Sonja went to Heaven. I'm sure she went there. If good people can go to Heaven, why shouldn't good cats and other good animals go to Heaven?

Although our home is now empty of cats, traces—and memories—of the cats remained long after they were gone. Bits of their hairs were to be found on the sofa and upholstered chairs, and rips from their claws were visible in the rugs and back of the sofa and chairs. My well-used desk, which already had nicks and scratches from years of wear and tear, was further adorned with a goodly number of cat claw rips.

Since I did not do a very good job of covering up his scratchings, the guest bathroom still shows the result of Thomas ripping his claws into the wooden cabinets and door frames when he first arrived at our home. In the garage, behind some boxes, I found dried-up clumps of hairballs, probably from Sonja because Thomas didn't care to roam in the garage.

When Dulcie and I were caring for our cats, we were also looking out for our friends in the backyard—the birds and ducks and squirrels and rabbits, and sometimes racoons, who discovered our place was a good place for a handout. Once two young racoons followed Dulcie around the backyard for a handout and were satisfied only when she threw them a couple of Twinkies.

The prime feeding place for our feathered friends was—and still is—a large white pine tree. Several birdfeeders hang from its outstretched limbs, and at the foot of the tree lies an old soup bowl used as a receptacle for tablescraps.

Since the feeders are filled every day and since not all tablescraps are thrown into the garbage bag, there is always a lot of wildlife traffic around the majestic pine tree.

Our family room has a large glass door which gives us a full-range view of the backyard. We can stand in the family room and watch the wildlife satisfy their hunger, and also enjoy the colorful flower gardens and the fruit trees and dogwood trees.

One fall day a few years ago, I chanced to look out to the backyard from the family room and saw a large black cat devouring the morsels I had placed in the soup bowl. Probably a new cat in the neighborhood making the rounds to see if it could find a place to hang around for some extra treats. When I knocked on the glass door to draw its attention, the cat looked in my direction and ran out of the yard.

A few days later the black cat was back again, eagerly consuming the scraps we had put out for the birds.

"Look at that cat; it's eating everything in sight," I said to Dulcie.

"Maybe it's hungry," she replied.

"Nah, it's not hungry. See how big it is. It looks well fed."

The black cat was as large as our Thomas was in his prime. I reasoned that the stranger just toured the neighborhood for food, and once it found some extra goodies it went back home for its regular meals.

When the black cat began making a daily habit of stealing the birds' tablescraps—it even ate stale bread—I decided to put a stop to its mooching. I fitted a piece of heavy cardboard in the midst of some pine tree branches and placed a supply of scraps on the board, satisfied that the cat would not find the new feeding spot.

Surprise! Surprise!

The next morning I found the cardboard, slightly warped, lying on the ground beside the pine tree. The tidbits of food were gone, of course. Either I did a lousy job of rigging the cardboard, or the cat was really hungry. Dulcie suggested that I was right on both counts.

If the black cat was so hungry that it climb a tree

*The black cat—Ben was his name—just before he was reunited with his owner after being lost for seven months.*

in search of food, then the poor animal must really be starving. We decided to feed the cat whenever we saw it on our property.

That was easier said than done. When I spotted the cat by the soup bowl I'd take it some food, but the moment the cat saw me, it ran out of the yard. The cat was obviously afraid of people, especially me anyway, so I decided the best thing would be just to leave the food in the dish and see if it would return. The cat did return, approaching the dish cautiously, but sometimes the dish would be empty, its contents having already been eaten by the scavenging blue jays and crows. This scenario went on for weeks, and I began to worry about the cat's safety and health because winter was approaching. While we seldom have snow in the tidewater region of Virginia, we do encounter some cold days during the late fall and winter season. The black cat obviously was a stray, but at one time it had an owner; it had been cared for, because it wore a white flea collar.

One December morning when I went out to the driveway to pick up my newspaper, I saw the black cat curled up and sleeping on a pile of leaves lying up against the east end of my neighbor's house. Protected against the wind by surrounding shrubs and warmed by the bright sun rays, the cat looked like a picture of contentment.

I approached it slowly. When the cat became aware of my presence it awoke and raised its head. I stopped.

"Well, hello, Blackie," I said. "Having a nice nap?"

The cat stared at me. It stayed in its place, making no attempt to run as it usually did when I approached it in the backyard.

"Come here, kitty." I moved closer to the cat. It meowed and arose and sought cover behind the shrubs. It made no attempt to run away.

"Hang on, Blackie. I'll get you something to eat."

I went into the kitchen and got a couple pieces of bologna to give to the cat. When I returned with the food, the cat was sitting in a hunched position behind the shrubs. Holding the bologna in my outstretched hand, I attempted to coax it to come to me, but the cat sat motionless behind the shrubs. Finally I tossed some pieces of meat on the grass near our fence.

"Come and eat it," I said. "I'm not going to bother you."

After I had had my breakfast and read the morning paper, I went out front of the house to check on the black cat. It was gone and so was the food that I had left.

Several days later I again saw the back cat resting by my neighbor's house. I approached it slowly and spoke softly to it. The cat remained still and seemed to be listening. I offered to bring it some food.

This time I tossed a few scraps of food into the grass in front of the cat, then made a trail of bits of food into our backyard, ending by the back door. I coaxed the cat toward the food, but it didn't move. I went back into the hose and waited. An hour later I went out to check on the cat and the food. The food was gone, and so was the cat.

Blackie—I decided that probably was its name—was gone for several days; when it reappeared, I tried the same food trail experiment again, with the same result. Was I making progress in befriending a lost cat, or was the black cat playing games with me—eating my food in the daytime and going to his proper home at night?

The next time I made contact with the black cat, I tried a new experiment. Instead of making a trail of food to lure it into the backyard, I showed it some food I held in my hand, then cajoled it to follow me to the back door of the garage and waited. And waited and waited. It didn't take the bait. I gave up and went inside the house. Several hours later I went out to see what had happened to the food. It was gone.

One day as I opened the back door, I spotted the black cat peeking at me from the rear corner of the garage. It was almost hidden from sight, because on that side of the house we have an azalea garden. The closely-planted azalea shrubs made a good hiding place for the cat.

"Well, hello, again," I said to Blackie. "Looking for another handout?"

To my surprise it answered with a loud meow.

I got some food and placed it on the walkway by the back door, then stepped inside to watch from behind the glass-paned storm door.

Soon the cat came into view. It approached the food cautiously, took a few bites, then ran off to hide among the azalea bushes. This process was repeated several times until all the food was eaten. With the food gone, the cat disappeared.

The cat returned the next day for more food, but it would be at least another week of this grab-it-and-run game before the black cat was confident enough to eat the food in one sitting before running away.

I also began opening the rear storm door and standing with half my body outside to watch the cat eat. At first it backed off when I opened the door, but when it realized that I wasn't going to do it any harm, it continued to eat. Obviously hungry, the cat gulped the food and nervously glanced from side to side as it was eating. When finished, it went into hiding in the azalea bushes.

One day I placed a saucer of milk beside the food as the black cat was watching me from the rear corner of the garage. I decided to stand outside the door.

*Ben, the lost cat, looks for a handout.*

"Come and get some milk, Blackie," I said. "Bet you haven't had any milk in a long time."

The cat approached slowly. It gulped some food, smelled at the saucer, then began eagerly lapping up the milk.

While the cat was eating, I noticed that its white flea collar contained some writing. As the cat busily drank the milk, I edged step by step slowly toward it until I was close enough to lean over to read the writing. It was a telephone number.

The cat ate the food, emptied the saucer of milk, and left for the day. I went into the house and telephoned the number written on the cat's flea collar.

A woman answered. I introduced myself.

"Do you own a black cat?" I asked. "A cat that has your telehone number on its flea collar?"

"Yes, we did, but it got lost," she answered.

I told the woman that the black cat had been hanging around our house for months, and that we were feeding it, but that it would disappear once it had been fed.

The woman was very happy to hear that her cat was alive. She said the cat, whose name was Ben, had disappeared shortly after her family had moved into their new home in July—it was now Janaury.

We were both surprised when she told me where she lived. Her house was on the next street—a mere five minutes' walk from my home!

Well, Blackie—I mean, Ben—must really have become confused and disoriented when he slipped away from his new home. His owner said that for four months she and her family criss-crossed the neighborhood searching for their lost Ben. They checked regularly with the SPCA and the city animal control office for their missing cat. They even checked with the police department to learn if Ben had been involved in any car accident.

The next morning about ten o'clock, the time when the black cat usually showed up for its feedng, Ben's owner arrived with a pet carrying case. Ben was resting on the pile of leaves up against the neighbor's house.

It was a happy reunion. Ben ran to his owner, meowed loudly and rubbed up against her legs. Ben was so excited that he drooled. They were both very happy and thankful. Ben also rubbed up against my legs as to say thanks for looking out for him. He also let me pat his head—and to think that for months he wouldn't let me come within an inch of him.

Ben protested loudly when I put him in the pet carrier, but he calmed down when I placed the carrier in his owner's car. I guess he knew he was going home.

The last I heard about Ben was that he showed no desire to venture outside his home. He was content to sit by the glass door and look into the garden.

### THE END

### MEOW MEOW